THE APOSTOLIC DEFENCE OF THE GOSPEL

THE APOSTOLIC DEFENCE OF THE GOSPEL

CHRISTIAN APOLOGETIC IN THE NEW TESTAMENT

by

F. F. BRUCE, D.D.

*Rylands Professor of Biblical Criticism and
Exegesis in the University of Manchester*

INTER-VARSITY PRESS

INTER-VARSITY PRESS
Inter-Varsity Fellowship
39 Bedford Square, London WC1

© The Calvin Foundation 1959

First British Edition	*December 1959*
Reprinted	*December 1961*
Second Edition	*June 1967*
Reprinted	*June 1970*

ISBN 0 85110 306 5

Made and printed in England by
STAPLES PRINTERS LIMITED
at their Rochester, Kent, establishment

CONTENTS

ACKNOWLEDGEMENT

Scripture quotations from the Revised Standard Version of the Bible (copyrighted 1946 and 1952 by the Division of Christian Education, National Council of Churches, U.S.A.) are used by permission.

INTRODUCTION

'ALWAYS be prepared to make a defence to anyone who calls you to account for the hope that is in you, yet do it with gentleness and reverence' (1 Pet. iii. 15).

These words, addressed by the apostle Peter to his fellow-Christians in Asia Minor, around the year 63, at a time when their faith was being exposed to a severe test, may serve as the New Testament authority for Christian apologetic. The very word which is rendered 'defence' in our quotation is *apologia*, the word from which 'apologetic' is derived. It is the word used by Paul in Philippians i. 7, 16, where he speaks of himself as being put in prison 'for the defence of the gospel'.

The second century AD is the period specially known as 'the age of the apologists'. It was the age when Christian leaders began to fight back against the repressive policy of the Roman state, regarding the pen as a mightier and worthier weapon than the sword. In the earlier part of that century we have the apologetic writings of Quadratus and Aristides; we have those of Justin Martyr in its middle years, while Minucius Felix and Tertullian bring up the rear at its close.

Christianity, said these second-century apologists, is innocent of the charges of sedition and immorality brought against it. It is preposterous indeed that honest and law-abiding people should be falsely accused of crimes and vices which have been freely ascribed to the gods worshipped by their accusers!

Christianity, they added, is the final and true religion by contrast with the imperfection of Judaism and the error of paganism. Not only does Christianity provide the proper fulfilment of that earlier revelation of God given through the prophets of Israel in Old Testament times; it also supplies the answer to the quests and aspirations expressed in the philosophies and cults of the other nations. It was divinely intended from the beginning to be a universal religion.

So, with varying emphases, they argued. But the main lines of apologetic argument found in their writings were already laid down in the first century; they are plainly to be recognized in the New Testament. It is with this New Testament apologetic that we are to concern ourselves in the following chapters. And it may be that a study of New Testament apologetic will help us to discover lines along which the defence of the faith should be conducted in our own day, when necessary allowances have been made for the differing situations of the first and twentieth centuries.

But in polemic and apologetic, as in every other form of Christian witness, the object must always be to commend the Saviour to others. A victory in debate is a barren thing compared with the winning of men and women to the cause of Christ. If at times we are inclined to forget this, the Christian apologists of the first century will refresh our memories.

They will remind us, too, that while Jesus remains the same, and the gospel is unchanging, the means adopted to defend the faith may vary widely according to the situation in which the apologist finds himself and the public with which he is confronted. The New Testament apologists were men who had understanding of the times; the kingdom of God calls loudly for such men today.[1]

---

[1] The contents of this book were delivered as five lectures under the Calvin Foundation in Grand Rapids, Michigan, in April 1958.

CHAPTER I

THE GOSPEL CONFRONTS JUDAISM

THE gospel confronted Judaism when Jesus entered into debate with synagogue-leaders in Galilee and with scribes and Pharisees in the temple courts in Jerusalem, as also when Jesus stood before the Sanhedrin and assured them not only that He was the Messiah (if that was the term they preferred Him to claim) but that they would see His vindication at the hand of God and witness His visitation in judgment. He and His claims constituted a threat to the 'establishment' in Judaea, and their own interests, as they saw the situation, demanded that He be got rid of.

I. THE APOSTOLIC PREACHING

But, far from getting rid of Him, they soon found that they were being confronted afresh by His claims, in a form which proved remarkably intractable. The followers of Jesus, who might have been expected (considering their panic-stricken behaviour when He was arrested) to disappear into the Galilaean obscurity from which they had come, returned to Jerusalem and began a campaign of public propaganda in support of the Messiahship of their recently crucified Master.

Jesus is the long-expected Messiah, they proclaimed; the prophetic scriptures which foretold Messiah's coming have been fulfilled by the ministry, suffering and triumph of Jesus, and the mighty works which He performed were so many 'signs' that in Him the messianic age had arrived.

The argument from prophecy and the argument from miracle were regarded by first-century Christians, as by their successors in the second and many following centuries, as the strongest evidences for the truth of the

gospel. Today they are more often felt to be an embar-
rassment, partly no doubt because they represent an
attitude to the Old Testament and a world-view which
are out of harmony with dominant modes of contemporary thought. And it may be part of our apologetic
task to convince people of our day that (as Jesus said to
the Sadducees) they are wrong, because they 'know
neither the scriptures nor the power of God' (Mt.
xxii. 29). It is necessary to inculcate a new awareness of
the authority of the Scriptures as God's Word written,
and a new awareness of the supernatural—of God at
work in the world which He created.

In the proclamation of the apostles the argument from
prophecy and the argument from miracle coincided and
culminated in the resurrection of Jesus. This was the
supreme messianic sign, the greatest demonstration of
the power of God, and it was at the same time the conclusive fulfilment of those prophecies which pointed to
the Messiah. Not only so, but it was something to which
the apostles could bear direct testimony. 'This Jesus God
raised up, and of that we all are witnesses' (Acts ii. 32).

By raising Jesus from the dead, they affirmed, God
had kept His promise to give His people the 'holy and
sure blessings' pronounced upon David and his line (Is.
lv. 3, quoted in Acts xiii. 34)—holy and sure blessings
which included the assurance that great David's greater
Son would not be abandoned to Hades and that His
flesh would not see corruption (Ps. xvi. 10, quoted in
Acts ii. 25 ff., xiii. 35). No-one else had been thus
delivered from death : Jesus therefore was indubitably
the Messiah, enthroned at God's right hand in accordance with the oracle of Ps. cx. 1 (Acts ii. 34 f.); He was
the obedient Servant of the Lord, exalted and extolled
and made very high after His submission to unmerited
suffering and death (Is. lii. 13 ff., quoted in Acts
iii. 13 ff.). Let those who had previously failed to
acknowledge Him now make haste and repent; if they
did, their sins would be blotted out and the blessings of
the messianic age would yet be theirs.

This was the confident burden of the apostolic message in its earliest days. The defence of the gospel at this stage was a defence of Jesus' claim to be God's Son and Messiah—a claim all too hastily disallowed by the chief priests and elders of the Jewish people, but now confirmed by the act of God, as the apostles could testify from their own experience.

No doubt the argument from Jesus' resurrection was peculiarly strong at a time when it could be maintained by men who had actually seen Him 'alive after his passion' and heard from the lips of the risen Lord an interpretation in all the Scriptures of 'the things concerning himself'. But Christians today may also emphasize the evidence for His resurrection as a most potent argument for the truth of Christianity; and their evidence will be the more effective if the power of His life is at work in their lives in such a way that others take note of it.

II. THE OFFENCE OF THE CROSS

But many of the apostles' hearers among the Jews were conscious of an insuperable difficulty. How could the crucified one be the Messiah? From every point of view but the apostles', the crucifixion of Jesus must have constituted a handicap when they spoke of Him in public, and in fact an account had to be given of His crucifixion in every phase of Christian witness and apologetic. To Jews the crucifixion of Jesus was a formidable obstacle in the way of believing Him to be their appointed Messiah; how could the Messiah, on whom the blessing of God rested in a unique degree, have died the death on which the curse of God was expressly pronounced? It was written plainly in the law : 'a hanged man is accursed by God' (Dt. xxi. 23). That Jesus came under the description 'a hanged man' was undeniable; but it was blasphemous to suggest that one who so clearly was 'accursed by God' could be Israel's Messiah.

The apostles from the earliest days of their preaching appear to have met this objection head-on; when describing the manner of Jesus' death, they seem deliberately to have selected language which would remind their hearers of that terrible sentence in the law. In their defence before the Sanhedrin, when they were charged with infringing the ban on teaching in Jesus' name, they said : 'The God of our fathers raised Jesus whom you killed *by hanging him on a tree*' (Acts v. 30). And Peter, telling the story of Jesus to Cornelius and his household, said : 'They put him to death *by hanging him on a tree*' (Acts x. 39). The apostles were well aware of the implications of being hanged on a tree; yet this did not make them hesitate for a moment in proclaiming that the one who had been so hanged was Lord and Messiah, Prince and Saviour. This proclamation they based upon the fact that God had raised Him from the dead; whatever significance might be attached to the form of death which He had died, it must be subject to the undoubted significance of His resurrection.

To Paul, in the period preceding his conversion to Christianity, the manner of Jesus' death was probably his conclusive argument against the disciples' claims. Jesus had died under the curse of God, and therefore could not be the Messiah; those who said He was, were self-convicted as blasphemers and impostors. But when Paul in his turn saw the risen Lord, he was immediately convinced that (contrary to his former belief) He was indeed the Messiah, the Son of God. His death by crucifixion did not have the implication that Paul thought it had. Yet the fact that the Messiah suffered an accursed death must have some extraordinary implication, and that implication is set out by Paul in what is probably the earliest of his extant writings. The curse pronounced in Dt. xxi. 23 is paralleled by another curse pronounced later in the same book : 'Cursed be he who does not confirm the words of this law by doing them' (Dt. xxvii. 26). Now, says Paul, 'all who rely on works of the law are under a curse; for it is written, "Cursed be every one who does not abide by all things written in the book of the law, and do them." . . . Christ redeemed us from the curse of the law, having become a curse for us—for it is written, "Cursed be every one who hangs on a tree"—that in Christ Jesus the blessing of Abraham might come upon the Gentiles, that we might receive the promise of the Spirit through faith' (Gal. iii. 10, 13 f.).

That is to say, Christ, by bearing the curse of God in one form (death by crucifixion), liberated His people who were under that curse in another form (through failure to keep the whole law of God), and secured for them the blessings of the gospel. This solution of the problem may well have taken shape in Paul's mind sooner rather than later in the period following his conversion, as the whole of his thinking became re-orientated around a new centre. Whether a similar solution presented itself to the earlier apostles cannot be said with certainty, but they must surely have found some satisfactory explanation of the paradox that the Messiah's enemies had been permitted to put Him to death 'by hanging him on a tree'.

In a well-known summary of the preaching which was common ground to the other apostles and himself, Paul gives first place to the affirmation that 'Christ died for our sins in accordance with the scriptures' (1 Cor. xv. 3). This affirmation—part of the primitive Christian tradition which Paul claims to have 'received'—not only states the accepted fact that Jesus died, but by saying that '*Christ* died' states that the one who died was the Lord's Anointed. It adds that His death was endured for His people's sins, and that in dying thus He fulfilled the sacred scriptures. Which scriptures? Pre-eminently, no doubt, though not exclusively, the scriptures which describe the suffering and death of the obedient Servant of the Lord as 'he bore the sin of many' (especially Is. lii. 13-liii. 12).

The apostolic preaching was obliged to include an apologetic element if the stumbling-block of the cross was to be overcome; the *kerygma,* to use our contemporary jargon (which we do the less reluctantly because it is also Pauline Greek), must in some degree be *apologia.* And the *apologia* was not the invention of the apostles; they had all 'received' it—received it from the Lord. To begin with, the cross had been a stumbling-block to themselves, until He appeared to them in resurrection and asked the question : 'Was it not necessary that the Christ should suffer these things and enter into his glory?' (Lk. xxiv. 26). Necessary indeed, because thus it was written; and so 'beginning with Moses and all the prophets, he interpreted to them in all the scriptures the things concerning himself' (Lk. xxiv. 27). And Paul, who had 'received' this account of the death of Christ among the things 'of first importance', was able accordingly in later days to tell a Jewish king that in his apostolic ministry he said 'nothing but what the prophets and Moses said would come to pass : that the Christ must suffer, and that, by being the first to rise from the dead, he would proclaim light both to the people and to the Gentiles' (Acts xxvi. 22 f.).

III. ISRAEL'S UNBELIEF

But if Jesus was indeed Israel's promised Messiah, and if His death (perplexing as it must appear at first sight) was so plainly foretold in Israel's sacred Scriptures, why did Israel for the most part refuse to recognize Him?

This was a further aspect of 'the Jewish problem' which early Christian apologetic had to face, and it was an aspect which did not emerge first in the apostolic age, for it was present in the course of Jesus' public ministry. The Synoptic and Johannine Gospels alike show an acute awareness of it. Mark, at an early stage in his Gospel narrative, records five controversial encounters of Jesus with the religious leaders of the people in such a way as to give the reader an impression of the early beginning and rapid development of a conflict which reached its climax with the crucifixion (Mk. ii. 1–iii. 6).

Jesus Himself drew attention to the failure of most of His hearers to believe His message or recognize the implications of His presence and ministry in their midst, and pointed out that history was repeating itself, because their ancestors had similarly failed to accept what God had to say to them through His servants the prophets. Isaiah, for example, was warned at the beginning of his prophetic career that his message, delivered by actions as well as words, would address itself fruitlessly to unseeing eyes and unhearing ears, and so it proved (Is. vi. 9 f., quoted in Mk. iv. 12). Isaiah's hearers professed lip-allegiance to God, but their hearts were far from Him, preferring their own ideas to the Word of God; and similarly the religious leaders of Jesus' time made the Word of God in effect a dead letter by the tenacity with which they held their own traditions, preferring them to the liberating message of the divine kingdom (Is. xxix. 13, quoted in Mk. vii. 6 f.). 'The stone which the builders rejected' had for long been proverbial in Israel; but the proverb had never had such point as now, when the Owner of the vineyard had sent His Son to receive its seasonal fruit, and the custodians of the vineyard had set upon that Son with murderous intent (Ps. cxviii. 22 f., quoted in Mk. xii. 10 f.). This parable at least was no riddle to those for whom it was meant : they knew very well that the vineyard of the Lord of hosts was the house of Israel (Is. v. 7), and 'they perceived that he had told the parable against them' (Mk. xii. 12).

It is striking how regularly the book of Isaiah is appealed to when the problem of Israel's unbelief is being dealt with in the New Testament, and it is plain that this use of that book goes back to Jesus Himself. In Luke's account of the parable of the vineyard the rejected stone of Ps. cxviii. 22 is identified with the stumbling-stone of Is. viii. 14 f., on which many will fall and be broken, and also with the stone cut out without hands of Dn. ii. 34 ff., which pulverized the grandiose structure of pagan world-dominion and replaced it by the kingdom of God (Lk. xx. 17 f.). A further link is

added to this chain of 'stone-testimonies' by Paul and
Peter in the sure foundation-stone of Is. xxviii. 16, laid
by God in Zion (Rom. ix. 33; 1 Pet. ii. 6), and that in
contexts where both apostles are dealing with the problem of those who stumbled at the gospel of Christ
instead of accepting it by faith. 'They stumble because
they disobey the word,' says Peter, *'as they were destined
to do'* (1 Pet. ii. 8). How destined? By the word of God
in the prophetic scriptures, and particularly in the book
of Isaiah.

IV. STEPHEN'S DEFENCE

Here we may turn to consider one quite distinctive
exposition of the problem of Israel's unbelief—the
speech of Stephen in Acts vii.

This speech is commonly called 'Stephen's apology';
but we should observe what kind of apology it is.
Although it was delivered before a court of law, by a
man on trial for his life, it is no forensic defence. Anything less likely to win a verdict of 'not guilty' from the
judges can scarcely be imagined. It is rather an apology
in the sense that it is a reasoned defence of the position
which he had maintained in the Hellenistic synagogue
which he attended in Jerusalem, and it may be regarded
as a sample of Christian Hellenistic apologetic against
Jewish objections to the gospel. ('Hellenistic', in this
context, has reference to Greek-speaking Jews; according to Acts vi. 1 ff. there was an influential body of these
'Hellenists' in the primitive Jerusalem church.)

Stephen, one of the leaders of the Hellenistic section
in the Jerusalem church in the years immediately following its inception, was gifted with an exceptionally keen
insight into the implications of the gospel for the status
of Judaism in the purpose of God. If the gospel was
true, then there was no more place for Judaism. The
old order and the new were incompatible. The apostles
might continue to live as observant and respected Jews,
attending the temple services in Jerusalem; but Stephen

saw that the gospel meant the setting aside of the temple order as a way of approach to God. As he expounded this thesis in the synagogue with eloquence and persuasive charm, he aroused fierce opposition on the part of those Jews who venerated the temple order, and was brought before the Sanhedrin on a charge of blasphemy —blasphemy against God and Moses. Against God, because (according to his accusers) he taught that Jesus of Nazareth would destroy Israel's holy place, where God dwelt among His people. Against Moses, because he taught that Jesus of Nazareth would change the customs which one generation had passed on to another since the time when Moses received them from God at Sinai.

The Sanhedrin had attempted in vain to pin the charge of speaking against the temple on Jesus Himself; the case of Stephen gave promise of greater success. Moreover, if Stephen could be convicted on this charge, the Sanhedrin knew that they would have the people of Jerusalem on their side. The apostles might enjoy popular goodwill to an extent which had made it unwise thus far for the Sanhedrin to proceed to extreme measures against them; but if they, and the community which they led, could be implicated in this charge brought against Stephen, a telling blow would be struck against them.

Stephen, invited to answer the charge, defended his teaching by an appeal to Old Testament history.

The Jerusalem temple, he said, was not of the essence of true religion. God had manifested His presence outside the frontiers of the Promised Land—to Abraham in Mesopotamia, to Joseph in Egypt, to Moses at Sinai. And long before any sanctuary was constructed for the God of Israel, all that was necessary for His worship existed.

When at last a sanctuary was constructed for Him, it was a mobile tent-shrine, as was fitting for a pilgrim people, who must always be ready, like their forefather Abraham, to pull up their stakes and move on when the signal was given. Not until the reign of Solomon was an immovable house built to be God's dwelling-place in the midst of Israel. But the disadvantage of such a house was that people were tempted to think that God could be confined within a temple made with hands, so that they had Him where they wanted Him. They were warned against this false attitude, but the warning fell on deaf ears. Solomon might say in his dedicatory prayer, 'Behold, heaven and the highest heaven cannot contain thee; how much less this house which I have built!' (1 Ki. viii. 27). And God might enforce the same lesson through His prophets :

> Heaven is my throne
> and the earth is my footstool;
> what is the house which you would build for me,
>   and what is the place of my rest?
> All these things my hand has made,
>   and so all these things are mine.
>
> (Is. lxvi.1f.)

But the people paid no heed; the temple was a talisman in which they put their trust instead of putting it in the living God. Jeremiah, in his great proclamation at the temple gate, urged the people to turn from this delusion : 'Do not trust in these deceptive words : "This is the temple of the Lord, the temple of the Lord, the temple of the Lord" ' (Je. vii. 4). Otherwise, he warned them, the temple in Jerusalem would meet the same fate as the sanctuary at Shiloh had suffered in earlier days.

And now Stephen, on whom the mantle of Jeremiah had fallen, warned his hearers against putting in the second temple the same false trust as their forefathers had put in the first one. He did not expressly foretell the destruction of the second temple, but its destruction might easily be inferred from his words; in any case, what Jesus had said in this regard was probably not unknown to the Sanhedrin. But the call of God to His people now was to leave the imagined security of their traditional cultus and go forth, like Abraham, wherever

God might lead. (It is not by accident that Luke presents the Gentile mission of the Church as the immediate sequel to Stephen's ministry.) The people, however, like their ancestors in the wilderness, wished to look back rather than to go forward. The charge of speaking against God came well from people whose ancestors had consistently rebelled against Him, from the worship of the golden calf in the wilderness on to the worship of the planetary bodies in later days! The present generation showed itself eager to follow the example of earlier generations in refusing to pay heed to the call of God.

And the charge of speaking against Moses came well from people whose ancestors had consistently repudiated Moses and killed the prophets, people who themselves had now filled up the measure of their fathers by repudiating and killing the Righteous One to whom Moses and the prophets had pointed forward!

Stephen's defence becomes an attack, delivered in the true prophetic vein. One can well imagine the sort of reply which might have been made to him by a pious Jew of the stamp of Ben Sira, the author of Ecclesiasticus, who dwelt on the bright side of his people's history rather than on the dark side. But Stephen was not addressing an audience of pious Jews like Ben Sira; he was addressing the very court which, only a few years before, had sentenced to death the Lord of the prophets. By their act, the people whom they represented had brought their age-long opposition to God and His messengers to a head by the rejection of Christ.

Here, then, we have an early sample of Hellenistic Christian apologetic against the Jew. In the next generation echoes of it are heard in the Epistle to the Hebrews, and in the next generation again further echoes are heard in the Epistle of Barnabas. Indeed, echoes of it are heard even in the strictest Hebrew Christian circles after the fall of the temple in AD 70. For the fact that God permitted the temple to be destroyed led a number of Hebrew Christians, who had up to that time retained a veneration for it, to the conclusion that God could never have intended the sacrificial ritual to be instituted in the first place. But Stephen, speaking thirty years before the Jewish war broke out, was not influenced in his thinking by the events of that war, but by the logic of the fact of Christ.

V. THE COMING RESTORATION

Stephen's defence contains no note of hope for the nation which had rejected God's word through the prophets in earlier days and had now crowned their rebellion against Him by rejecting His Son. But the situation could not be left there, for if it were, a grave problem in theodicy would arise.

Among Stephen's opponents was 'a young man named Saul' who was as convinced as Stephen was that the old order and the new were incompatible. But whereas Stephen's conclusion was that, since the new had come, the old must go, Saul's conclusion was that, since the old must not be imperilled, the new must go. Not long after Stephen's trial and death, however, Saul of Tarsus underwent the revolutionary change which turned him from the most active persecutor of the new order into its most energetic champion. To him, the old order now assumed the appearance of a temporary dispensation ordained by God until the time came for the fulfilment of the promises made to Abraham and the other patriarchs centuries before the giving of the law. He recognized as fully as Stephen did the tragic implications of Israel's failure to welcome the One in whom the promises of God were fulfilled. But the tragedy lay principally in this, that the people of Israel might have been expected to be foremost in giving Him a welcome, since it was among them pre-eminently that God had prepared the way for the coming of the Saviour. 'They are Israelites,' he writes, 'and to them belong the sonship, the glory, the covenants, the giving of the law, the worship, and the promises; to them belong the patriarchs, and of their race, according to the flesh, is the Christ' (Rom. ix. 4 f.). The patriarchs had received the promises, which were to be fulfilled to their descendants; the patriarchs' descendants repudiated the fulfilment of the promises when it came.

But did this mean that God's purpose had been frustrated? Did it mean that He had rejected His own people? Far from it! First of all, it was evident from the Old Testament narrative that God had always followed the plan of selecting some for the furtherance of His purpose, and passing over others. Again, it was equally evident from the Old Testament narrative that Israel had shown itself 'a disobedient and contrary people' long before the coming of Christ (Is. lxv. 2, quoted in Rom. x. 21); in their refusal of Christ they were not adopting a totally unprecedented attitude to the revelation of God. But throughout Israel's history there had always been a believing and obedient remnant, and so it was now. Paul provided evidence enough in his own person that God had still reserved for Himself 'a remnant, chosen by grace' (Rom. xi. 5). The existence of such a remnant, now as previously, guaranteed the realization of God's purpose; through the present remnant Israel's divinely appointed mission to spread the knowledge of God among the Gentiles was being accomplished, as the gospel was proclaimed to all the nations.

But what of the majority of Israelites, who had not accepted the Messiah? Could one simply label them 'vessels of wrath made for destruction' and leave the matter there? Some might be content to do just that, but not so Paul. It was true that their present rejection of the gospel was not only in keeping with their forefathers' conduct, but was in fact the fulfilment of specific Old Testament predictions. Their unbelief had been explained centuries before by Isaiah, when he said: 'God gave them a spirit of stupor, eyes that should not see and ears that should not hear, down to this very day' (Is. xxix. 10, quoted in Rom. xi. 8). Paul understood their plight very well, for he himself had at one time been overpowered by this 'spirit of stupor' until his eyes

were opened and his ears unstopped on the Damascus
road. But this sad state of affairs was not to last for ever.
The hardening of heart which had befallen Israel had
even now affected only part of the people, albeit the
more numerous part; and with regard to the part
affected by it, it was only temporary. God in His wisdom
had so ordered matters that this partial and temporary
hardening of Israel was the occasion for the swift and
wide-scale spreading of gospel blessings among the
Gentile nations. The sequel to this blessing of the Gentiles
would be the promotion of God's ultimate purpose for
all Israel. For God had said through Moses : 'I will make
you jealous of those who are not a nation; with a foolish
nation I will make you angry' (Dt. xxxii. 21, quoted in
Rom. x. 19). And the full significance of these words
would appear when unbelieving Israel, seeing the outpouring of God's blessing on the Gentiles, would be
moved to jealousy. 'These blessings are ours by right,'
they would say; 'why should these Gentiles enjoy them
while we are shut out from them?' Thus shaken out of
their spirit of stupor, they would see and hear aright,
and claim Christ and the gospel for themselves. Addressing Gentile believers, Paul sums the situation up thus :
'Just as you were once disobedient to God but now have
received mercy because of their disobedience, so they
have now been disobedient in order that by the mercy
shown to you they also may receive mercy. For God has
consigned all men to disobedience, that he may have
mercy upon all' (Rom. xi. 30-32). Thus Paul, rising to
the height of his great argument, solves the problem in
theodicy raised by Israel's unbelief in a manner which
does justice to every principle of the gospel : *sola gratia,
sola fide, soli Deo gloria.*

Meanwhile, the bringing of gospel blessings to the
Gentiles is itself a theme of Old Testament prophecy,
and thus we are introduced to our next study, the
defence of the gospel in relation to paganism.

The defence of the gospel to the Jewish world of

today is a duty which still rests on Christians, but it is a
much more delicate responsibility in the twentieth
century than it was in the first. The Christian witnesses
who commended the gospel to the Jews of New Testament days did so with clean hands. Christians today
must recognize with humility and repentance that nothing could have been less calculated to commend the
gospel to Jews than the attitude adopted towards them,
generation after generation, by people who professed
and called themselves Christians. There is substance in
the charge of a well-known rabbi : 'Christendom has
hidden the face of Christ from us.'

In the present century the Jewish people have passed
through a greater tribulation than any that they have
ever been called upon to endure—at the hands of a
system which was as inherently (though not as murder-
ously) anti-Christian as it was anti-Jewish. With this
consummation of the 'connatural' understanding of
suffering which they have accumulated throughout the
centuries, it could be that they will find less difficulty in
recognizing in Jesus as the Suffering Servant One who,
afflicted in His people's affliction, is the hope and
salvation of Israel.

CHAPTER II

THE GOSPEL CONFRONTS PAGANISM

I. TO THE GREEKS FOOLISHNESS

IF the proclamation of Christ crucified was a scandal to pious Jews, it was foolishness to sensible Gentiles, and especially to those Gentiles who were self-consciously the heirs of Greek culture. To them the cross of Christ was not a theological problem, but it was a practical obstacle in the way of their taking the gospel seriously. How could they be expected to accept as Deliverer, Leader and Lord One who had neither the wisdom nor the power to save Himself from such a hideous death?

Christian apologists of the first century made no attempt to gloss over the fact of the cross so as to make their message more palatable to their Gentile audiences. On the contrary, they placed it in the forefront of their message and accepted the situation that, by all the recognized standards of wisdom and power, Christ crucified was a spectacle of foolishness and helplessness. But nonetheless, through Christ crucified God had achieved what all the recognized forms of wisdom and power had proved unable to achieve—the redemption of men and women who were formerly enslaved to sin. And this showed clearly that the recognized standards of wisdom and power were not God's standards. 'For the word of the cross is folly to those who are perishing, but to us who are being saved it is the power of God. For it is written, "I will destroy the wisdom of the wise, and the cleverness of the clever I will thwart." Where is the wise man? Where is the scribe? Where is the debater of this age? Has not God made foolish the wisdom of the world? For since, in the wisdom of God, the world did not know God through wisdom, it pleased God through the folly of what we preach to save those who believe. For Jews demand signs and Greeks seek wisdom, but we preach Christ crucified, a stumbling-block to Jews and folly to Gentiles, but to those who are called, both Jews and Greeks, Christ the power of God and the wisdom of God. For the foolishness of God is wiser than men, and the weakness of God is stronger than men' (1 Cor. i. 18-25).

Thus spoke the chief defender of the gospel in the apostolic age. And with such a defence the gospel presented as direct a challenge to pagan philosophy as it did to the law of Judaism.

II. THE ATTACK ON IDOLATRY

If even the highest manifestation of pagan culture was challenged by the gospel, much more did it challenge those manifestations which were specially offensive in the eyes of monotheistic Jews and Christians—the various forms of pagan idolatry. Here, if anywhere, we see how the defence of the truth involves the exposure of error.

Pagan religion was offensive because it worshipped many gods instead of one, worshipped gods that were no gods but rather demons, worshipped gods that were represented by visible and tangible images. Pagan religion was idolatrous to the core. More sophisticated minds among the pagans might point out that the image was not the deity, but only a representation of the deity; but to less sophisticated minds—and that means the great majority of pagans—the idol embodied the deity's personality to such a degree that the two were identified : to all intents and purposes the idol *was* the deity, and as such received the direct worship of its devotees.

In its attitude towards idolatry, the New Testament perpetuates a tradition which reaches far back into Old Testament times. Elijah on Mount Carmel mocked the frantic prophets of Baal who called upon their god to hear them, because he knew that their god was no god.

Speaking of the heathen, a Hebrew psalmist says :

> Their idols are silver and gold,
>   the work of men's hands.
> They have mouths, but do not speak;
>   eyes, but do not see.
> They have ears, but do not hear;
>   noses, but do not smell.
> They have hands, but do not feel;
>   feet, but do not walk;
>   and they do not make a sound in their throat.
> Those who make them are like them;
>   so are all who trust in them.
>   (Ps. cxv. 4-8; cf. Ps. cxxxv. 15-18.)

And the classical exposure of idolatry in the Old Testament is the passage in Is. xliv. 9-20, which depicts a man choosing a good tree and felling it. Part of the wood he uses to light a fire to cook his food and warm himself; then, when he is fed and warmed, he turns his mind to higher things and uses the remainder of the wood to fashion an image, before which he falls down in adoration, saying : 'Deliver me, for thou art my god!'

This tradition is carried on in Hellenistic Jewish literature such as the Letter of Aristeas and the Book of Wisdom, and it is continued after New Testament times in the apologists of the second Christian century. In the New Testament itself it finds clearest expression in Rom. i. 18-32, Paul's great indictment of paganism. Paul makes it clear that idolatry is not merely the worship of idols in the form of graven or molten images; the essence of idolatry is the worship of a created thing instead of the Creator. And, even as the writer of the Book of Wisdom asserts that 'the idea of making idols was the beginning of fornication, and the invention of them was the corruption of life' (Wisd. xiv. 12), so Paul traces the proliferation of pagan immorality in his day back to the time when men first 'exchanged the glory of the immortal God for images resembling mortal man or birds or animals or reptiles' (Rom. i. 23). (The number of parallels between the Book of Wisdom and the first two chapters of Romans led the late Ronald A. Knox to suggest, in playful mood, that a thesis might be written to show that Wisdom was written by Paul himself before he became a Christian!)

Paul emphasizes, moreover, that in forsaking the true knowledge of God the pagan world was inexcusable, for the knowledge of God was accessible to them both in the works of creation without and in the voice of conscience within. But Paul goes beyond others who had presented a similar indictment against pagan idolatry and immorality by weaving his indictment into a more comprehensive pattern in which pagan and Jew are brought together as equally guilty before the bar of divine righteousness.

The Epistle to the Romans, however, is written to Christians; in his indictment of paganism in its opening chapter Paul is preaching to the converted. There are two passages in Acts where the gospel is shown in direct confrontation with paganism, and these two passages anticipate the main line of second-century Christian apologetic against the pagans. They are the passages which record Barnabas and Paul's protest against idolatry at Lystra (Acts xiv. 8-18), and Paul's address before the court of the Areopagus at Athens (Acts xvii. 16-34). The gospel confronted unsophisticated pagans in the former place, sophisticated pagans in the latter.

III. PAGAN WORSHIP AT LYSTRA

During their joint missionary campaign in Cyprus and Asia Minor—a campaign based on the great Gentile church of Syrian Antioch—Barnabas and Paul visited the Roman colony of Lystra, a city of the region of Lycaonia in the province of Galatia. There Paul cured a man who had been a cripple from birth. The indigenous, non-Roman population of Lystra were so excited at the spectacle that they concluded that their city was being favoured with a visitation from divine beings. In local legend Zeus, the supreme god, and Hermes his herald had once visited that district *incognito;* and in fact there is archaeological evidence of a joint cult of Zeus and Hermes in that area lasting well into the Christian era. Here, said the people, were those two deities again; Barnabas was Zeus, and Paul, who was always foremost in speaking, was obviously Hermes. But if such exalted visitants had come to Lystra, they must be treated appropriately, and preparations were made to offer Barnabas and Paul divine honours, the priest of Zeus Propolis (Zeus whose temple lay in front of the city gates) taking it upon himself to make a solemn sacrifice of oxen.

As the animals were being decked with woollen garlands as a preliminary to being sacrificed on the altar, the two apostles suddenly realized what was afoot. They had not grasped the situation at first, because the inhabitants were talking in their Lycaonian vernacular, which the apostles did not understand. But now they rushed out into the midst of the crowd with every sign of horror and consternation, and urged them to stop what they were doing at once. Not only did they deprecate the payment of divine honours to themselves, but they improved the occasion by trying to show the folly of all idolatry and to lead their hearers to the knowledge of the true God.

'Men,' they cried, 'what is this you are doing? We are only human beings, made up exactly like yourselves; but we have come to bring you good news. You must turn away from this futile worship and seek the living God. He is the God who made heaven, earth and sea and everything that is in them. In the ages that are past He has allowed all the nations to follow their own ways, and yet He has not left Himself without any hint of His being and character; for He sends you from heaven rain and fruitbearing seasons, and fills your hearts with food and joy.'

Reluctantly the men of Lystra desisted from their sacrificial proceedings, and a few of them even went so

far as to pay heed to the further implications of the
apostles' words.

Instead of the arguments from prophecy and miracle,
which were so freely used when the gospel confronted
Judaism, the apostles on this occasion appealed to God's
natural revelation as Creator and Sustainer of the
universe, to His 'common grace' in fact. The seasonal
rainfall, the regular harvests which not only kept them
alive but filled them with good cheer—all these things
were the gift of the living God whom they did not know.
Why not give up the worship of those futile divinities
who never did anything for them, and render grateful
acknowledgement to the real God to whom they owed
life and livelihood?

It has often been pointed out that there are strong
resemblances between Luke's summary of the apostolic
preaching at Lystra and Paul's account of the way in
which his converts at Thessalonica became Christians.
'You turned to God from idols,' he says, 'to serve a living
and true God, and to wait for his Son from heaven,
whom he raised from the dead, Jesus who delivers us
from the wrath to come' (1 Thes. i. 9 f.). To be sure,
these words contain a more positive Christian content
than anything recorded in the preaching at Lystra, but
the preaching at Lystra provides the first stage in the
presentation of the gospel to pagans (a stage which was
unnecessary in its presentation to Jews), and is exactly
calculated to make them 'turn to God from idols, to
serve a living and true God'. In the next stage they
would be told how the God who created all things and
made temporal provision for those whom He created
also made provision for their redemption by sending His
Son from heaven.

Although no explicit reference is made in the preaching at Lystra to the Old Testament revelation, yet the
preaching is full of Old Testament echoes. The way in
which the living God is introduced as He 'who made
the heaven and the earth and the sea and all that is in
them' is practically a quotation from the Decalogue

(Ex. xx. 11). The description of pagan deities and cults as 'vanities' or 'futilities' is thoroughly in accord with Old Testament usage, both in the Hebrew original and in the Greek Septuagint. God's providential kindness in sending rainfall and harvest is a recurrent Old Testament theme (cf. Gn. viii. 22), and the conjunction of 'food and gladness' as gifts from God has also Old Testament parallels (cf. Ec. ix. 7).

That God 'in past generations . . . allowed all the nations to walk in their own ways' implies that He has exercised a certain forbearance hitherto which now, with the advent of the gospel age, has come to an end. This is brought out more explicitly in Paul's speech at Athens, where he speaks of God as having 'overlooked' the former 'times of ignorance' but as now commanding 'all men everywhere to repent' in view of the final revelation which He has given of Himself in Christ (Acts xvii. 30). To this later and fuller speech we must now turn our attention.

IV. PAUL BEFORE THE AREOPAGUS

Probably no ten verses in the New Testament have supplied the text for a greater abundance of commentary than that which has grown up around Paul's *Areopagitica* (Acts xvii. 22-31). Diametrically opposing views have been expressed on the question whether Paul did deliver, or indeed could have delivered, such a speech as is summarized in these verses. It is noteworthy that classical students who have studied the speech in its setting are prominent among the champions of its genuineness; here, if anywhere in the New Testament, students of classical antiquity feel themselves to be on home ground, and to them the whole passage rings true. Of those scholars who cannot accept it as an authentic utterance of Paul's, probably the majority feel that it is too unlike those places in the Pauline Epistles which treat of the same subjects : some of these points will come up for discussion in what follows.

Paul's debates in the Athenian *agora* with those who

were willing to enter into argument with him—adherents
of the main philosophical schools among others—excited
some interest. He laid such stress on Jesus and His
resurrection that some of his hearers, who cannot have
paid very careful attention to what he said, imagined
that he was recommending the worship of two new
deities—*Iesous* and his consort *Anastasis* (words which
they perhaps interpreted as 'Healing' and 'Restoration').
But a man who was introducing a new religion came
under the jurisdiction of the Areopagus, the most
venerable court in Athens, which enjoyed great prestige
because of its antiquity and took specific cognizance of
certain moral and religious questions. Before this court,
then, Paul was brought—probably in the 'Painted Colon-
nade' which was its customary meeting-place in these
days. He was not required to defend himself as though
he were on trial for some offence; he was rather invited
to expound his teaching before the body which was
responsible to decide whether it contravened public weal
or not.

As at Lystra, so before the Areopagus, Paul does not
expressly quote Old Testament prophecies which would
be quite unknown to his audience; such direct quotations
as his speech contains are from Greek poets. But he does
not argue from the sort of 'first principles' which formed
the basis of the various schools of Greek philosophy; his
exposition and defence of his message are founded on
the biblical revelation of God, and they echo the thought
and occasionally the very language of the Old Testament. Like the biblical revelation itself, his speech begins
with God the Creator of all, continues with God the
Sustainer of all, and ends with God the Judge of all.

He finds his point of contact in an altar-dedication
which illustrated the intense religiosity of the Athenians
—a quality which impressed many other visitors to their
city in ancient times. This altar-dedication read : TO AN
UNKNOWN GOD. Other writers inform us that altars to
'unknown gods' were to be seen at Athens, and various
tales were told to account for their erection. One of these

tales told how they were set up by the direction of
Epimenides, a wise man of Crete, some centuries before
this time; it is possibly significant in this regard that
Epimenides is one of the poets from whom Paul quotes
in the course of his speech. Whatever the original circumstances or intention of this particular inscription
may have been, Paul used it as a text on which to hang
his address. 'You acknowledge that you do not know
the nature of God,' he said, 'in the very act of paying
Him worship; since you confess your ignorance of His
nature, I have come to tell you the truth about it.' Paul
does not exactly say, as the King James Version suggests,
that the God to whom the altar was dedicated is the
God whom he proclaims; he uses the neuter gender :
'What therefore you worship as unknown, this I proclaim to you' (Acts xvii. 23).

(*a*) Paul proceeds, then, to instruct them in *the
doctrine of God*. Firstly, God is the Creator of the
universe and all that is in it; He is Lord of heaven and
earth. This is undoubtedly the God of biblical revelation; the very language is distinctively biblical. No
concessions are made to the ideas of Hellenistic
paganism; no distinction is made between the Supreme
Being and a 'demiurge' or master-workman who
fashioned the material world because the Supreme Being
was too pure to come into contaminating contact with
matter.

Secondly, God does not inhabit shrines which human
hands have built. Stephen had to impress this upon the
Sanhedrin with reference to the Jerusalem temple, built
for the worship of the living God; much more had Paul
to impress it upon the Areopagus with reference to the
glorious temples of the Athenian Acropolis, dedicated to
gods that were no gods. The higher paganism, indeed,
had realized that no material structure could accommodate the divine nature, but the affinities of Paul's
language to this effect are biblical and not classical.

Thirdly, God requires nothing from His creatures.
Here too, parallels to Paul's argument can be adduced

from classical Greek literature, but Paul stands right within the Hebrew prophetic tradition in this as in other features of his exposition. The prophets found it necessary to refute the idea which so many of their Hebrew contemporaries cherished, that God was in some degree dependent upon them and their gifts. The truth was that they were completely dependent on Him, but He was completely independent of them. This is how the God of Israel speaks in Ps. l. 9-12 :

> I will accept no bull from your house,
> nor he-goat from your folds.
> For every beast of the forest is mine,
> the cattle on a thousand hills.
> I know all the birds of the air,
> and all that moves in the field is mine.
> If I were hungry, I would not tell you;
> for the world and all that is in it is mine.

And this is precisely Paul's emphasis here, when he declares that the God who made the world and everything in it, seeing He is Lord of heaven and earth, receives no tendance from human hands as though He were in need of anything. Far from men's supplying any need of His, it is He who supplies every need of theirs : to them all He gives 'life and breath and everything'.

(*b*) The Creator of all things in general is the Creator of mankind in particular; and this consideration leads Paul on from the doctrine of God to *the doctrine of man*.

Firstly, man is one. The Greeks might take pride in their innate superiority to barbarians; the Athenians might boast that, unlike their fellow-Greeks, they were autochthonous, sprung from the soil of their native Attica. Paul, on the contrary, proclaims that all mankind is one in origin, all created by God and all derived from a single common ancestor. Before God, we meet on one level. It is hardly necessary to point out the relevance of this truth today : the biblical doctrine of man demolishes all fancied justification for claims to superiority based on class, race or colour.

Secondly, man's earthly abode and the course of the seasons have been divinely ordained for his benefit. This, too, is a biblical insight. According to the first chapter of Genesis, the earth was formed and furnished to be man's home before man himself was introduced as its occupant. And part of the forming and furnishing of man's home on earth consisted in the regulation of the 'allotted periods'—probably to be identified with the providential sequence of seed-time and harvest (as in the speech at Lystra) rather than with the appointed epochs for the rise and fall of nations (as in the visions of Daniel).

Thirdly, God's purpose in making these arrangements was that man might seek and find Him. We may compare Paul's statement in Rom. ii. 4, 'God's kindness is meant to lead you to repentance.' The question how man came into a position where he needed to seek and find God does not come to expression here, but the answer need not remain in doubt when we remember the biblical foundation of Paul's speech and his account of man's first disobedience in Rom. v. 12 ff. It is clearly implied throughout the speech that the ignorance about the divine nature admitted by the Athenians and shared with them by others is a culpable ignorance.

Fourthly, God's desire that men should seek and find Him is the more natural because they are His offspring, and He aids them in the attainment of His desire by His nearness to them. It is here that the terminology of this speech shows closest Hellenistic affinities, but to another audience Paul might have expressed the same thoughts in more biblical terminology by saying that man is God's creature, made in His image. To his present audience he establishes his point by two quotations from Greek poets which set forth man's relation to the Supreme Being.

The first quotation is the fourth line of a quatrain attributed to Epimenides the Cretan, in which Zeus, father of gods and man, is addressed thus :

They fashioned a tomb for thee, O holy and high one—
The Cretans, always liars, evil beasts, idle bellies!
But thou art not dead; thou livest and abidest for ever,
For in thee we live and move and have our being.[1]

The second quotation comes from the poem on
Natural Phenomena by Aratus of Cilicia. This poem
opens with a passage about Zeus—Zeus the Supreme
Being of Greek philosophy rather than Zeus the amoral
head of the Greek mythological pantheon :

Let us begin with Zeus; never let us leave him unmentioned,
O mortals. All the roads are full of Zeus and all men's
meeting-places; the sea and the harbours are full of him. In all
our ways we all have to do with Zeus; *for we are also his
offspring.*

In introducing these quotations, did Paul intend to
identify the Zeus of Greek philosophy with the living
God of the Bible? Or did he simply detach from their
original context words which could be easily adapted to
his essentially biblical context, in spite of possible
protests that the poets whom he quoted had meant by
these words something quite different from what he
made them mean? It is, in fact, quite consistent with
Paul's outlook to allow that these writers expressed
thoughts which, despite the pagan contexts in which
they were conceived, indicated a real if limited appre-
hension of the true God. A Christian preacher today
may quote the well-known lines about prayer from
Tennyson's *Morte d'Arthur* without subscribing either to
the ideals of the Arthurian legend or to Tennyson's
religious position :

More things are wrought by prayer
Than this world dreams of. Wherefore, let thy voice
Rise like a fountain for me night and day.

[1] The second line of the quatrain will be recognized as the testimony of a Cretan 'prophet' quoted in Tit. i. 12.

For what are men better than sheep or goats
That nourish a blind life within the brain,
If, knowing God, they lift not hands of prayer
Both for themselves and those who call them friend?
For so the whole round earth is every way
Bound by gold chains about the feet of God.

Man, then, is God's offspring; in the order of creation man's life is lived 'in God'. The argument that this speech cannot come from Paul, since it teaches a 'God-mysticism' whereas his Epistles teach a 'Christ-mysticism', fails to distinguish things that differ. The term 'mysticism' is inappropriate in both regards, and especially in regard to the teaching of the *Areopagitica*. But, apart from that, it would have been pointless to talk to a pagan audience about the significance of being 'in Christ'. Here Paul is dealing with men's relation to God in the old creation, not with that redemptive relation which men of the new creation enjoy 'in Christ Jesus' as 'sons of God, through faith' (Gal. iii. 26). His present concern is to impress on his hearers the responsibility of all men, as God's creatures into whom He has breathed the breath of life (Gn. ii. 7), to give Him the honour which is His due. This honour is not given when men represent the divine nature under material forms. Again we hear echoes of the biblical polemic against image-worship : 'we ought not to think that the Deity is like gold, or silver, or stone, a representation by the art and imagination of man' (Acts xvii. 29).

Fifthly, Paul issues a call to repentance. The Athenians were quite right in acknowledging their ignorance of the divine nature. This ignorance was not entirely without blame; Paul implies here what he emphasizes in Rom. i. 19 ff., that if men had paid heed to God's works in creation, they might have found sufficient testimony there to His everlasting power and divinity. But, culpable as their ignorance was, God in His mercy passed it over. There is a parallel here not only to the statement in the speech at Lystra that God had hitherto 'allowed all the nations to walk in their own ways' (Acts xiv. 16) but also to Paul's teaching in Rom. iii. 25 about God's forbearance in the passing over of sins committed in former times. In all these places it is implied that the coming of Christ means a fresh beginning. The particular point here is that God has overlooked men's earlier ignorance of Himself in view of the final revelation which He has now given of Himself in Christ. His overlooking of their former ignorance was a token of patience, not of indifference. But now that the knowledge of God is available in the gospel, let all men forsake their ignorance and accompanying disobedience and turn to the true God who has come near to men in Christ.

For God the Creator of all is also God the Judge of all. Already by His own authority He has appointed a day in which 'he will judge the world in righteousness' (Acts xvii. 31)—a thoroughly biblical expression. Greek cyclic theories of history made no room for a true eschatology. Greek writers might picture men who in their lifetime were eminent for justice—Minos, Aeacus and Rhadamanthys—as meting out judgment in the realm of the dead; but such a picture is essentially different from Paul's proclamation that the righteous judgment of the world of which the psalmists spoke (cf. Pss. ix. 8, xcvi. 13, xcviii. 9) will be accomplished by God through Jesus Christ at a fixed epoch in the future. How thoroughly Pauline the conception is may be gathered from several places in his Epistles—e.g., from Rom. ii. 16, where he speaks of 'the day when, according to my gospel, God judges the secrets of men by Christ Jesus'.

The 'man whom he has appointed' to consummate His eternal purpose is no doubt the 'one like a son of man' of Dan. vii. 13, who receives this authority from the Ancient of Days. The Fourth Evangelist may reproduce this Semitic idiom when he says that the Father has given the Son 'authority to execute judgment, because he is the Son of man' (Jn. v. 27). But this idiom would be meaningless to the members of the Areopagus;

hence Paul expresses the same sense in plain Greek.

Moreover, says Paul, God has given a pledge to mankind that Jesus is the One ordained to judge the world in righteousness in that He has raised Him from the dead. Here we have a New Testament anticipation of the theme more recently popularized in the writings of Dr. Oscar Cullmann, that V-Day is guaranteed by D-Day—that the final consummation of victory is guaranteed by the fighting and winning of the decisive battle in the campaign, no matter what length of time elapses between that battle and the end of the campaign.

Paul's speech at Athens strikes one as an admirable introductory lesson in Christianity for cultured pagans. He leads his hearers from their self-confessed ignorance of the divine nature to the point where the Man of God's appointment is introduced. The second lesson might well begin where the first one stopped, and explain who this Man was and why He was raised from the dead. For the rest, the introductory lesson is an exposition of the true knowledge of God, set forth as no merely intellectual discipline, but as something involving moral and religious responsibilities. The knowledge of God, as Paul presents it, is the knowledge of God of which the Old Testament speaks : it is rooted in the fear of God; it belongs to the same spiritual order as truth, goodness and covenant-love; for lack of it men and women perish; it will cover the earth when God's will is perfectly done and His eternal covenant finally established. The 'delicately suited allusions' to Stoic and Epicurean tenets which have been recognized in the speech, like the quotations from the pagan poets, have their place as points of contact with the audience, but they do not commit the apologist to acquiescence in the realm of ideas to which they originally belong. Unlike some later apologists who followed in his steps, Paul does not cease to be fundamentally biblical in his approach to the Greeks, even when (as on this occasion) his biblical emphasis might appear to destroy his chances of success.

For the note of the resurrection of the body, on which he ended, was thoroughly uncongenial to his hearers' minds. Had he replaced it by the Greek doctrine of the immortality of the soul, all but the Epicureans who listened to him would have agreed with him. But the Greek attitude to resurrection is well expressed by the words which Aeschylus ascribes to Apollo on the very occasion when the court of the Areopagus was founded : 'Once a man dies and the earth drinks up his blood, there is *no resurrection*' (the word is *anastasis*, the word so constantly on Paul's lips). So, when Paul spoke of resurrection, the majority of his hearers paid him no further attention; only a few took his message seriously. But the true Christian apologist will not compromise or dilute the gospel to make it more palatable to those whom he wishes to persuade of the truth of Christianity.

The twentieth-century apologist, in confronting contemporary paganism, especially in the western world, will find it necessary to expose erroneous ideas for what they are. He must remove obstacles which lie in the way of people's accepting the truth—false beliefs about God, for example. He must not try to accommodate the gospel to them, for all his endeavour to present it in an idiom understood by his hearers or readers. He will, however, be vigilant to seize upon every appropriate point of contact. Anything that rings a bell in his hearers' minds may serve, for their minds are full of questions and aspirations—sometimes only half-consciously realised— to which the answer and fulfilment are provided by the gospel.

Like his first-century predecessors, the apologist of today must confront men with the truth about God— Creator, Provider, Lord of history, Judge of all—and His command to repent. He must confront them with the truth about man, and his moral bankruptcy in the sight of God. And above all he must confront them with Jesus Christ in His resurrection power, His authority to execute judgment, and His redeeming love by which He delivers men and women from their estrangement and rebellion and creates them anew in the knowledge of their Creator.

CHAPTER III

THE GOSPEL CONFRONTS THE ROMAN EMPIRE

I. TRIBUTE TO CAESAR

IN those days', says Luke the Evangelist, introducing his narrative of the birth of Jesus, 'a decree went out from Caesar Augustus that all the world should be enrolled' (Lk. ii. 1). If his purpose was to fix the date of our Lord's birth by reference to a contemporary incident in imperial history, he has not achieved complete success, for there is no agreement on the date of the particular enrolment to which he refers.

But probably Luke's purpose is much wider than the fixing of date. He deliberately sets the two rulers over against each other. Caesar Augustus has established his supremacy over the Roman world; it is in token of that supremacy that he decrees a world-wide census. In certain parts of his empire there was a custom that on such an occasion a man must go to his family home to be registered there. We have evidence of this custom in Egypt; according to Luke, it was observed in Judaea too. For, in response to the imperial will, 'Joseph also went up from Galilee, from the city of Nazareth, to Judaea, to the city of David, which is called Bethlehem, because he was of the house and lineage of David, to be enrolled with Mary, his betrothed, who was with child. And while they were there, the time came for her to be delivered' (Lk. ii. 4-6). And that is why Jesus was born in Bethlehem of Judaea.

Of course, the Christian reader of the New Testament today reads Luke's account with Matthew's parallel narrative in his mind, and he knows of another reason why Jesus was born in Bethlehem of Judaea; he remembers how the religious experts of Jerusalem told Herod the Great that the Messiah would be born in Bethlehem, because this was divinely foretold through the prophet Micah (Mt. ii. 5 f., quoting Mi. v. 2). But Caesar Augustus had no idea that his decree was but an instrument for the fulfilment of a more august decree than any of his.

What did Augustus know or care about the domestic inconvenience to which his edict might expose two or three of his humblest subjects in a remote frontier-province? The Child who was born in Bethlehem during that enrolment never came to his notice. He spent most of His life in obscurity, and not until after His death did He come to the notice of any Roman emperor, even in the most casual manner. Yet that Child was to constitute a challenge to successive emperors for nearly three centuries, until at last one emperor did what his predecessors had refused to do, and bowed in acknowledgement of the superior power of Mary's firstborn.

Luke, of course, wrote long before the time of Constantine; but even by the time when he wrote, two generations or so after the birth in Bethlehem, the challenge of Christ was forcing itself upon the attention of the Caesars. And Luke has this in his mind when he records the connection between the decree of Augustus and the incarnation of the Son of the Highest.

The whole issue raised by the emperor's enrolment policy was hotly debated in Israel during the earlier years and public ministry of Christ. Was it proper for Israelites to acknowledge the sovereignty of a pagan ruler by paying him the tribute which he imposed as the sequel to the enrolment? There were some Israelites who maintained that it was quite improper; God alone was Israel's King, and to pay tribute to a pagan monarch who did not acknowledge the true God was an act of treason not only against the nation but against high heaven. Foremost among these were the Zealots, so called because they showed themselves zealous on God's behalf, like Phinehas the priest in the early days of the nation's history (Nu. xxv. 13). They maintained the ideals and policies of Judas the Galilaean, who 'arose in the days of the census' in AD 6, when Judaea was reduced to the status of a Roman province and was required to pay tribute directly to Rome (Acts v. 37). And it was they who played a prominent part in the Jewish revolt against Rome which broke out in AD 66 and led to the destruction of the temple and city of Jerusalem four years later.

It was thus no merely academic question that was posed to Jesus by a group of Pharisees and Herodians in the temple court in Jerusalem : 'Is it lawful to pay taxes to Caesar, or not? Should we pay them, or should we not?' (Mk. xii. 14 f.). If He said 'No', He could at once be denounced to the Roman authorities for sedition; if He said 'Yes', He would forfeit popular good will, for (like political extremists in many other places and periods) the Zealots were regarded by many of the rank and file as being the truest patriots. Jesus' answer, in effect, was : 'The money is Caesar's in any case; it bears his name and likeness. Let him have back what so plainly belongs to him. But don't forget to render to God, your heavenly King, what belongs to *Him*.'

The incident is intelligible enough against the background of Zealot agitation. But, as with so many things recorded in the Gospels, it is useful to ask not only what its setting was in the life of Jesus, but what its setting was in the life of the early Church—that is to say, what led to its being remembered and recorded. And it is most probable that this incident played an important part in the apologetic of primitive Christianity because it underlined the Christians' claim that there was nothing disloyal about their faith and worship; that they were lawabiding subjects of the emperor, acknowledging his undoubted rights.

The spirit of Jesus' words about the tribute money is echoed by Paul in Rom. xiii. 1-7, where he enjoins submission to the secular authorities, who serve God by protecting the law-abiding and punishing law-breakers. 'For the same reason', he adds (that is, for the sake of

Christian conscience), 'you also pay taxes, for the authorities are ministers of God, attending to this very thing. Pay all of them their dues, taxes to whom taxes are due, revenue to whom revenue is due, respect to whom respect is due, honour to whom honour is due' (verses 6, 7). It is perhaps significant that he should write so explicitly on this point to the Christians in Rome at a moment when he was planning a visit to the city.

In very similar vein Peter writes : 'Be subject for the Lord's sake to every human institution, whether it be to the emperor as supreme, or to governors as sent by him to punish those who do wrong and to praise those who do right. . . . Honour all men. Love the brotherhood. Fear God. Honour the emperor' (1 Pet. ii. 13 f., 17). Writing from Rome about AD 63, on the eve of a 'fiery trial', Peter impresses upon his readers in Asia Minor their duty to the imperial authorities, and no-one into whose hands the letter fell would have found any support in it for the common belief that Christianity was a seditious movement.

II. CHRISTIANITY AND ROMAN LAW

We must bear in mind that Christianity started off with a serious handicap in the eyes of Roman law. When the gospel confronted Judaism and paganism, the crucifixion of Jesus was a religious and intellectual stumbling-block; so far as Christian relations with the imperial power went, this was a tremendous political and juridical stumbling-block. It could not be denied that Christians were the followers of a Man who was crucified by the sentence of a Roman judge on a charge of sedition. Christianity thus stood branded as a movement whose founder was a convicted and executed criminal—a movement comparable to those led by Judas the Galilaean and Theudas the wonder-worker. When the historian Tacitus first has occasion to refer to Christians (in connection with the aftermath of the great fire of Rome in AD 64), he explains his reference by saying that 'they got their name from Christ, who was executed by the procurator Pontius Pilate when Tiberius was emperor' (*Annals,* xv. 44). The origin of the Christian name sufficed to indicate the sort of people that Christians were.

Moreover, as if to confirm this impression, Christianity was regularly attended by disorder as it made progress through the provinces of the empire. That this was so in the case of Paul's apostolic activity is clear to the reader of Acts. How some pagans regarded the progress of Christianity is shown by Tacitus, who goes on to say, after his reference to the execution of Christ, that by His execution 'the baneful superstition was checked for a short time, only to break out afresh, not only in Judaea, where the plague first started, but in Rome itself, where all the horrible and shameful things in the world collect and find a home'.

Paul might be blamed for the disorders which attended the advance of the gospel in Asia Minor, Macedonia and Greece, but he could not be blamed for the riots which broke out in Rome in AD 49, when Claudius was emperor. Suetonius says these riots were instigated by 'Chrestus' (*Life of Claudius,* 25); but that is just a confused indication of the fact that they resulted from the introduction of Christianity into the Jewish community in Rome. The sequel to these riots is mentioned by Luke in Acts xviii. 2, where we are told that Aquila and Priscilla came to live in Corinth about that time, 'because Claudius had commanded all the Jews to leave Rome'. And it has been argued that similar disorders troubled the Jewish community of Alexandria in Egypt in the reign of Claudius.

What answer could be given to the charge that Christianity was obviously illegal from the start, and that it provoked unrest and rioting wherever it appeared?

In the first place, it was pointed out that the condemnation of Jesus was a miscarriage of justice. The governor Pontius Pilate had sentenced Him to death, it was true, but he had pronounced that sentence reluc-

tantly and against his better judgment. Luke, in particular, tells how Pilate pronounced Jesus not guilty when
His accusers charged Him with 'perverting our nation,
and forbidding us to give tribute to Caesar, and saying
that he himself is Christ a king' (Lk. xxiii. 2 ff.). Even
when these charges were amplified, Pilate persisted in
his verdict of 'Not Guilty', and Herod Antipas, tetrarch
of Galilee, concurred with this assessment of the situation. It was the insistence of the Jewish chief priests, says
Luke, and the clamour of the city mob incited by them,
that forced Pilate at last to change his mind and pass
the death-sentence. Not only so, but one of the bandits
who were crucified along with Jesus told his companion
in crime that Jesus, unlike themselves, had done no
wrong—that is to say, He did not belong, as they did,
to a rebel organization operating against the occupying
power. And the centurion who commanded the detach-
ment of Roman soldiers charged with carrying out the
crucifixion remarked, when Jesus had breathed His last,
that He was certainly an innocent Man.

All these details help to build up a cogent *apologia*
against the *prima facie* impression which the average
citizen of the Roman Empire would receive when he
learned that the founder of Christianity had been sentenced to death by a Roman governor. But this is only
part of the defence of Christianity which Luke addressed
to the representatives of imperial law and order. Both
parts of his history of Christian origins have a strong
apologetic emphasis; if in the first part he rebuts the
charge that Jesus was personally a rebel against Rome,
in the second part he defends the Christian movement
in general against the accusation of provoking disorder
wherever it spread.

III. THE WRITINGS OF LUKE

Luke's avowed purpose in writing his twofold history
(which is preserved in the New Testament in the Third
Gospel and the Acts of the Apostles) was to provide one

Theophilus with a more trustworthy account of the beginnings of Christianity than anything he had previously received. The first part of his work is, by and large, a record of the apostolic witness to Jesus' ministry in word and action, death and resurrection. The second part takes up the tale with the resurrection of Jesus and carries it on for some thirty years; it traces the progress of the gospel from Jerusalem to Rome, and concludes with the principal herald of the gospel proclaiming it at the heart of the empire with the complete acquiescence of the imperial authorities.

As in his Gospel Luke exposes the illegality of the conviction of Jesus, so in Acts he introduces an impressive variety of people in official positions, both Gentile and Jewish, showing good will to Paul and other Christion missionaries, or at least admitting that the charges brought against them by their enemies lack any basis in fact. In Cyprus the proconsul Sergius Paulus gives a favourable reception to the apostles and their message (Acts xiii. 7, 12). At Philippi, a Roman colony, the chief magistrates apologize to Paul and Silas for subjecting them to illegal beating and imprisonment (Acts xvi. 37 ff.). At Corinth Gallio, proconsul of Achaia from AD 51 to 52, rules that the accusations of illicit religious propaganda, brought against Paul and his colleagues by the local Jewish community, relate to internal interpretations of the Jewish law, and he pronounces them guiltless of any offence against Roman law (Acts xviii. 12 ff.). At Ephesus the Asiarchs, distinguished citizens occupying positions of responsibility in the province of Asia, are friendly to Paul; and the chief executive officer of the municipal administration publicly absolves him of the charge of sacrilege or blasphemy against the established cult of the city (Acts xix. 31, 35 ff.). In Judaea the procurator Felix and his successor Festus find Paul innocent of the serious crimes of which he is accused by the Sanhedrin; the Jewish client king Agrippa II and his sister Bernice agree that he has done nothing deserving death or even imprisonment (Acts xxiv. 1 – xxvi. 32).

And when Paul exercises his right as a Roman citizen and appeals from the provincial court to the tribunal of the emperor in Rome, he carries on his missionary activity for two years in Rome itself, under constant military surveillance, without any attempt to hinder him (Acts xxviii. 30 f.). If Christianity was really such a lawless movement as was widely believed, Paul would certainly not have been allowed to propagate it by the imperial guards who had charge of him during his detention in Rome!

What was to be said, then, about the strife and disorder which so regularly attended the advance of Christianity? Luke answers this question by fixing the responsibility for the strife and disorder on the Jewish authorities. Just as it was the Jerusalem Sanhedrin that prosecuted Jesus before Pilate, so it was the same body that prosecuted Paul less successfully before Felix and Festus. And most of the disturbances which broke out when the gospel was carried from city to city throughout the Roman provinces were fomented by the local Jewish communities, who refused to accept the gospel themselves and were annoyed when their Gentile neighbours accepted it.

Where can we find an appropriate life-setting for a work which strikes the apologetic note in this particular way? To my mind there is none so appropriate as the situation in Rome in the sixties of the first century. Paul's arrival in Rome about the beginning of AD 60, his apostolic witness there for two years, the legal process involved in his appeal to Caesar—all this must have brought Christianity to the notice of several members of the official class in the city. Previously, if they knew of Christianity at all, they thought of it as another of those disgusting oriental cults which infected the lower orders of Rome as the sewers of the Syrian Orontes discharged themselves into the Tiber. But this man Paul was a Roman citizen, and his case had to be examined impartially and dispassionately. The title 'most excellent' which Luke gives to Theophilus (Lk. i. 3) probably marks him as belonging to the equestrian order—the second order in the hierarchy of Roman society. He was representative of the intelligent middle class of Rome, and Luke seized the opportunity to supply him and people like him with a more accurate and orderly account of the rise and progress of Christianity than they were likely to get elsewhere—and seized the opportunity, too, to vindicate the innocence of Paul and other Christians in relation to Roman law. How Luke thought of dedicating his narrative to this particular man we do not know; Theophilus may very well have been concerned in the preparations for the hearing of Paul's case by the emperor or his deputy. We can scarcely go so far as some, who suppose that Theophilus was the lawyer briefed for Paul's defence, and that Luke wrote his two-fold history in order to provide him with the information which he required for the conduct of the defence; there is much in Luke's history that would have been irrelevant for any forensic purpose, even if we conclude that the form in which we now have it represents a later and fuller edition than that of the sixties. None the less, Luke must be recognized as the pioneer in that type of apologetic which is addressed to the secular authorities in order to establish the law-abiding character of Christianity.

IV. THE APPEAL TO CAESAR

Paul's appeal to Caesar, to which reference has been made, deserves some further consideration. It was one of the privileges of a Roman citizen to appeal to the emperor against the decision of an inferior magistrate; or the appeal might be made (as it was in Paul's case) at an earlier stage in the proceedings if the defendant thought that he might not have justice done him in the inferior magistrate's court. Under the empire the appeal to Caesar represented the merging of two distinct rights which had existed in the days of the Roman republic : the right of any citizen to appeal to the sovereign people, and the right of a plebeian citizen to appeal to one of

the tribunes against the decision of any other magistrate.
Why did Paul exercise this right?

Firstly, no doubt, in the hope of securing in Rome the
justice which he feared he might not get in Judaea. The
new procurator, Festus, might allow himself through
inexperience to be influenced by the Jerusalem Sanhedrin to Paul's detriment. Paul had benefited on earlier
occasions by the impartial decision of Roman officials
whose judgment was not deflected by such influences;
in particular, he had good reason to be grateful for the
attitude of Gallio in Corinth. When the Jewish authorities in Corinth accused Paul of propagating a religion
which Roman law did not countenance, Gallio ruled, in
effect, that the religion which Paul propagated was a
form of Judaism, and therefore entitled to the recognition and protection which Roman law extended to
Judaism. Gallio has been held up as an awful warning
in sermons beyond computation because of the statement
in the King James Version that he 'cared for none of
these things' (Acts xviii. 17); but Luke is really com-
mending Gallio for his impartiality, not blaming him
for indifference to spiritual matters. Gallio's official
status and family connections were such that his ruling
would be adopted as a precedent by other magistrates.
The memory of this favourable decision may well have
encouraged Paul to appeal to Caesar, in the hope of
securing a decision equally favourable and even more
authoritative from the supreme tribunal of the empire.

Secondly, Paul may have hoped to win the emperor's
recognition of Christianity as a permitted cult—a *religio
licita*—in its own right, or as the true and proper fulfilment of the historic hope of Israel. Certainly, in making
this (or any other) move Paul was not the man to be
swayed purely by considerations of his personal safety.
The interests of the gospel were paramount with him,
and he confidently expected that these interests would
be promoted as a result of his appeal. He knew how, on
the day of his conversion, the Lord described him to
Ananias of Damascus as 'a chosen instrument of mine

to carry my name before the Gentiles and kings and the sons of Israel' (Acts ix. 15). His appeal to Caesar might give him an opportunity of bearing witness to Christ before the ruler of the Roman world. What if Caesar himself could be won for Christ?

And thirdly, his appeal to Caesar might hasten the fulfilment of the Lord's prerequisite condition for His *parousia* : 'the gospel must first be preached to all nations' (Mk. xiii. 10). Rome was the centre of the world; all roads led to Rome, and along these roads the gospel could radiate out from Rome in all directions, thus speeding the day when the full number of the Gentiles would come in and so all Israel would be saved.

Some of these aims were realized. Perhaps Paul did stand before Caesar and secure a favourable verdict. His two years' stay in Rome certainly reinforced the establishment of Christianity in the city, and therefore in the empire. But the position of Christianity in relation to Roman law, far from being improved by Paul's appearance before Caesar, was to deteriorate rapidly in the years immediately following. The situation in which Paul could count upon the protection of Roman law in his apostolic ministry was inevitably a temporary one, and came to an end in the early sixties. Gallio's ruling in AD 51 may have been adopted as a precedent by other magistrates for the following ten years or so, but it was decisively reversed by the imperial action against Christianity in AD 64, when the Emperor Nero found in the Christians of Rome convenient scapegoats for the charge of setting the city on fire.

V. THE FIERY ORDEAL

One reason for the change in situation between the fifties and the sixties was that it became increasingly difficult for Christianity to share the recognition which Judaism enjoyed at the hands of Roman law. It was both inevitable and desirable that Christianity should cease to be regarded as another variety of Judaism; indeed, Paul's evangelization of the Gentiles made it more and more evident that Christianity was not a distinctively Jewish movement. The Jews themselves would spare no pains to show that they did not recognize Christianity as a form of Judaism, and between AD 62 and 65 they had a powerful friend at court in Poppaea, who was empress during those years.

A second reason for the change was the general tendency to regard Christians as anti-social. Their avoidance of social activities which involved idolatry and the like was misinterpreted as due to 'hatred of the human race'. The disrupting effect of Christianity on family relationships, when some members of the family were believers and others were not, increased the dislike which was widely felt for Christians. Tacitus calls them 'a class of people loathed for their vices' and says that, when Nero tried to fix the crime of arson on them, a great number were convicted, not so much on this charge (which broke down on examination) but as enemies of humanity. He makes it clear that, in his opinion (and no doubt in the opinion of many others), even if they did not set Rome on fire, they fully deserved the most exemplary punishment because of their general character.

It was no longer sufficient for Christians to be told that if they did good, they would receive the approval of the secular authorities, as it had been when Paul wrote the Epistle to the Romans in AD 57. In the First Epistle of Peter, written six or seven years later, we can see the change taking place before our eyes. Peter enjoins upon his readers due obedience to the rulers and asks them : 'Now who is there to harm you if you are zealous for what is right?' (1 Pet. iii. 13). But in the same breath he mentions the possibility of their suffering for righteousness' sake, and goes on to warn them about a 'fiery ordeal' which is coming to test them—an ordeal in which any one of them may be called upon to suffer 'as a Christian' (iii. 14 ff., iv. 12 ff.).

In this new situation, in which Christians were liable

to suffer penalties imposed by Roman law just because they were Christians, Christian apologists continued to protest that they were innocent of any crime, but their protests went unheeded. In the second and third centuries those who voiced such protests were told that they might easily prove their loyalty to the empire by worshipping the state gods, and in particular by burning incense to the emperor's image or swearing by his divinity. Such actions were, of course, impossible for any conscientious Christian.

But the tendency to treat the emperor as being, for official purposes, a divine person existed already in the first century; it was bound up with an imperial ideology which constituted a third and specially powerful reason for the hostility towards Christianity which hardened throughout the Roman world in the second half of the century.

In this ideology Caesar was much more than the minister of God to execute His wrath on the evil-doer and make it possible for the law-abiding to lead quiet and peaceable lives without molestation. Caesar was the personification and deification of society, and claimed the total allegiance of his subjects. We have, in fact, the spectacle of two spiritual totalitarianisms confronting each other. The imperial ideology was inclusive and tolerant; provided that it received a modicum of recognition it allowed its votaries to please themselves to a great extent in the matter of other religious commitments. But on this point Christianity was exclusive; Christians worshipped God through Christ, and could not pay, or appear to pay, divine honours to anyone or anything else. Their total commitment to Christ imposed on them the obligation to be loyal subjects of the emperor and to pray for his welfare, but it forbade them to pray *to* him. (The Jews, in accordance with the first commandment, were similarly debarred by their religion from emperor-worship, but they had long enjoyed specific concessions in this matter from successive emperors.)

Just how completely opposed the two ideologies were

to each other may be gathered from Professor Ethelbert Stauffer's great work, *Christ and the Caesars*. He pays particular attention to the evidence of the imperial coinage (which was regularly used as a propaganda medium) in this regard. The imperial coinage is full of the characteristic motifs of Advent and Epiphany, celebrating the blessings which the manifestation of each successive divine emperor was to bring to a waiting world. Among the adulatory formulas with which the emperor was acclaimed, he mentions, as going back probably to the first century, 'Hail, Victory, Lord of the earth, Invincible, Power, Glory, Honour, Peace, Security, Holy, Blessed, Great, Unequalled, Thou Alone, Worthy art Thou, Worthy is he to inherit the Kingdom, Come come, do not delay, Come again' (p. 155). Indeed, one has only to read Psalm lxxii 'in Latin, in the official language of the empire, to see that it is largely the same formal language which is used alike in the Forum for the advent of the emperor and in the catacombs for the celebration of the Epiphany of Christ' (p. 251). Here there could be no compromise. Who was worthy to ascend the throne of the universe and direct the course of history? Caesar, or Jesus?

Domitian (AD 81–96) claimed divine honours more explicitly than any of his predecessors on the imperial throne; he was pleased to be called 'Our Lord and God' by his subjects. But Nero also received similar honours; the king of Armenia, for example, paid him homage as his 'master and god'. And we know how the Emperor Gaius in AD 40, indignant because the Jews would not recognize him as a god, ordered his statue to be erected in the temple at Jerusalem—an order which, even though it was countermanded, made the most solemn impression on Jews and Christians alike.

The Christian refusal to countenance such claims, and the language in which they ascribed divine honours to Jesus, could easily be given the appearance of sedition. Paul and his friends were accused before the city magistrates of Thessalonica in AD 50 of subversive activity and, in particular, of proclaiming a rival emperor, one Jesus (Acts xvii. 6 f.). It is to the credit of these magistrates that they did not panic when they heard this grave charge, but dealt with it firmly and moderately.

Later in that year Paul wrote a letter to the church which had been planted in Thessalonica during his brief visit to the city, and told them not to be misled by anyone who told them that the day of the Lord was upon them. Before that day came, he said, the principle of anarchy which was at present working secretly in the world would come into the open, incarnated in 'the son of perdition, who opposes and exalts himself against every so-called god or object of worship, so that he takes his seat in the temple of God, proclaiming himself to be God' (2 Thes. ii. 3 f.). This description echoes the words of Jesus about 'the abomination of desolation standing where he ought not' (see Mk. xiii. 14), reinterpreted in the light of Gaius' attempt ten years previously to have divine honours paid him in the Jerusalem temple. But for the present, Paul goes on, the manifestation of this 'man of lawlessness' is restrained by a power which will continue to exercise this restraint 'until he is out of the way' (see 2 Thes. ii. 7). The restraining power is probably the imperial authority as Paul knew it, a valued protection against the lawless forces which rose up to hinder the progress of God's work. But Paul thought it best to express his mind in veiled language; if his letter fell into the wrong hands, an explicit mention of the possibility that the imperial authority would be taken out of the way might have been regarded as confirmation of the charge of sedition brought against him in Thessalonica a few weeks before.

VI. THE APOCALYPSE

Of all the provinces of the Roman Empire, there was none in which emperor-worship was more thoroughly organized than in Asia. In the Asian city of Pergamum the cult of Rome and Augustus was established as early as 29 BC. Some think that John had this cult in mind when he described Pergamum as the place 'where Satan's throne is' (Rev. ii. 13)—although others think of the cult of Asklepios, the healing-god with his serpent-image, which was also located there. At any rate, in addition to the other forms of paganism with which Christians in the province of Asia had to live there was this specially seductive form. Coolness towards the imperial cult might be put down to lack of patriotism.

We remember how Paul had friends among the Asiarchs of Ephesus, who warned him not to enter the theatre when the riotous demonstration was being held in defence of the great goddess Artemis against her traducers. But it was from the Asiarchs—the leading men in the cities of the province of Asia—that the high priesthood of the imperial cult was recruited, and the Asian aristocracy thought it an honour to serve in this way. The temptation must at times have been strong for Christians to compromise just a little, to avoid giving their pagan neighbours the impression that they did not appreciate the blessings of peace and prosperity which the institution of the empire had brought to that part of the world. But the majority would not compromise, and to them the imperial cult proved a deadly enemy.

The Revelation of John reflects the situation of the Asian churches under the Flavian dynasty (AD 69–96). A fierce persecution of Christians—no doubt that of AD 64—has already broken out in Rome (Rev. xvii. 6), and in the province of Asia, too, the hostility of the authorities is directed relentlessly against the churches. This hostility John sees as initiated by the devil, the great red dragon, who wages war against the saints through two principal agents—the beasts of Revelation xiii. The former of these beasts, the beast from the sea (or abyss), is the imperial power; the other, the beast from the land (otherwise called the false prophet), is the imperial cult. The power which in Paul's time had operated as the minister of God now appears energized by the devil to destroy the people of God. Caesar has trespassed beyond his divinely allotted sphere and is claiming authority over 'the things that are God's'; and to this claim Christians can give no countenance.

What then is their defence, as the age-old enemy of God and His people stirs up the imperial power and the imperial cult to make war upon them? They conquered him, says John, 'by the blood of the Lamb and by the word of their testimony, for they loved not their lives even unto death' (Rev. xii. 11). They refused to compromise their allegiance to Christ, in spite of all the blandishments and threats of their enemies; they submitted to martyrdom, and their blood was like seed which produced a rich harvest in later generations. The victory which their Lord, 'the faithful witness', had already won was held up before them by John to encourage them to persevere in their own faithful witness, so that His victory might be theirs.

When Caesar encroaches on a sphere which is not his, as in fact he has been doing in so many places in our own day, Christians, who should be foremost in rendering to Caesar what he may rightfully claim, must be foremost in refusing his wrongful claims. For Christians recognize that Jesus Christ their Lord is 'the ruler of kings on earth', and therefore Caesar's ruler too. In the British coronation service a golden orb surmounted by a cross is presented to the sovereign with these words: 'When you see the orb set under the cross, remember that the whole world is subject to the power and empire of Christ our Redeemer.' Happy are those nations whose rulers acknowledge the Redeemer's crown rights.

And if as yet we do not see all things put under Him, we may at least bear witness that He is Lord. 'The patience and faith of the saints', which won the victory in the early Christian centuries, will do the same today, when new totalitarianisms, new imperial ideologies, rise up to claim the whole of life as their domain. Such a victory, in fact, is being won before our eyes by our brethren in other parts of the world who triumph through the blood of the Lamb and the word of their testimony, and are prepared to part with life itself sooner than forswear their allegiance to Christ. While such faithful confessors remain, no Christian need doubt the sure advent of that day when the kingdom of the world becomes 'the kingdom of our Lord and of his Christ, and he shall reign for ever and ever' (Rev. xi. 15).

CHAPTER IV

THE GOSPEL CONFRONTS PSEUDO-CHRISTIANITY

PSEUDO-CHRISTIANITY, as used in the title of this chapter, embraces a variety of 'Christian deviations'—to use a phrase recently popularized by Dr. Horton Davies—but deviations so radical that they deprive Christianity of its essential character, and can thus be set in contrast to 'Christianity rightly so called'. We shall look at four such perversions of pure Christianity which appeared in the first century AD, and consider the defence which was maintained against them. They are (i) Christianized legalism, (ii) Ascetic Gnosticism, (iii) Antinomian Gnosticism, and (iv) Docetism.

I. CHRISTIANIZED LEGALISM

By Christianized legalism is meant the attempt to combine the gospel of the grace of God with the legalistic principles of Judaism. Such attempts were made more than once in the history of the apostolic Church, but we may pay particular attention to the attempt which called forth from Paul his Epistle to the Galatians.

In the years AD 47 and 48 Paul and Barnabas engaged in a campaign of evangelism, based on Syrian Antioch, which included Cyprus and central Asia Minor in its scope. In the latter territory they met with special success in some of the cities in the southern part of the Roman province of Galatia, and churches were planted in these cities—notably in Pisidian Antioch, Iconium, Lystra and Derbe. But not long after the two missionaries returned to Syrian Antioch, trouble broke out in that church and spread to the recently planted churches of South Galatia.

The mother-church of Jerusalem included in its membership many Jewish believers who could be described as 'zealots for the law'. Some of them had affinities with the party of the Pharisees. To these men the church was little more than a group within the Jewish commonwealth—a group which cherished Jesus' fulfilment of the messianic hope, which their fellow-Jews had failed to recognize. They would agree that, since so many Jews had failed to recognize Jesus as the Messiah, a number of Gentiles had to be incorporated into the messianic community in order that the full quota of the elect of the last days might be made up. But these Gentiles had to be incorporated as proselytes; they were under an obligation not only to believe in Jesus as the Messiah but also to observe the Mosaic law. The twelve apostles did not accept this view, and no more did Paul and Barnabas. But these 'zealots for the law' looked for leadership not to the apostles but to James the Just, the brother of Jesus, although it must be said that James was a much wiser and more moderate man than these extremist followers of his.

A delegation of these men visited Antioch and tried to impose their views on the church there. For a time the situation was very delicate, because some Christian leaders at Antioch thought that temporary concessions should be made to these visitors' strong convictions; but Paul refused to concede an inch, because he believed that basic principles of the gospel were at stake, and his firm stand helped to rally the waverers.

The situation was more precarious in the churches of Galatia. These churches were visited by Judaizing Christians from Jerusalem, who insisted that the young Galatian Christians must submit to circumcision and undertake to keep the Jewish law if they were to win acceptance by God or recognition as fellow-believers by the Jerusalem church. In their inexperience the Galatian Christians were disposed to pay heed to the earnest representations of these visitors. Perhaps Paul was not so well informed as they had imagined; according to these visitors, he was a latecomer to Christianity and had not been directly commissioned by Jesus as the Jerusalem apostles were. If Paul had any authority at all, he received it from the leaders of the Jerusalem church; but these Judaizers could claim to represent the true faith as practised at Jerusalem.

The addition, however, of circumcision and other requirements of the Jewish law as necessary for salvation was not so much an addition to the gospel as a perversion of it. It nullified the principle that salvation is bestowed by grace and received by faith, and gave man a share in the glory of salvation which, according to the gospel, belongs to God alone. The whole scheme as proposed by these Judaizers was a different gospel from that which Paul and his fellow-apostles preached; it was, in fact, no gospel at all.

When news of what was happening in the Galatian churches came to Paul, he wrote an urgent letter to them, warning them, as they valued their salvation, not to give up the liberating message which they had heard from him and accept in its place a system which could only bring them into spiritual bondage. His defence of the gospel against the legalists makes the following points :

1. The gospel which Paul preached was one which he received by a direct commission from Christ. This involves him in a defence of his apostleship and a review of his movements from the time of his conversion (with special reference to his relations with the Jerusalem church), that it might be seen from the facts how baseless was the charge that he was indebted to the Jerusalem leaders for such authority as he possessed. Incidentally, Paul's defence of his apostleship, to which he repeatedly found himself driven in the course of his career, forms an interesting phase of Christian apologetic in the first century, although it is not one to which our present work pays detailed attention. But for Paul it frequently played a necessary part in his defence of the gospel.

2. If acceptance with God could have been attained by observing the old Jewish law, what (asks Paul) was the point of the death of Christ? He died for His people's salvation, but there was no need for Him to die if salvation could have been procured in the way indicated by the Judaizers.

3. Christian life (as the Galatian Christians knew from their own experience) is a gift of the Spirit of God; when they received it, they received at the same time unmistakable proofs of the Spirit's presence and activity in their midst. But if they began their Christian career on that high plane, was it not preposterous to imagine that they could continue it on the lower plane of legal works?

4. The Judaizers justified their insistence on the necessity of circumcision by appealing to the example of Abraham. Circumcision was the seal of the covenant which God made with him, and no uncircumcised person could hope to have a share in that covenant with all its attendant blessings. To this Paul replied that the true children of Abraham are those who are justified by faith in God, as Abraham was. Those who believe God, as Abraham did, enjoy the blessings promised by God to Abraham. God's promise to Abraham found its fulfilment in Christ, not in the giving of the law. The blessings which are embraced in that promise, then, are not obtained through Mosaic law (which was introduced long after the promise and could not modify its terms), but through faith in Christ.

5. The law pronounces a curse on those who fail to keep it in its entirety. Those who trust to the law for their salvation, then, are exposing themselves to the risk of this curse. But Christ, by His death on the cross, has delivered His people from the curse which the law pronounces; why then should they go back and put themselves under it anew?

6. The principle of righteousness by law-keeping belongs to the age of spiritual immaturity, the apron-string stage. But now that Christ has come, those who

place their faith in Him attain their spiritual majority as responsible sons of God. To listen to the arguments of the Judaizers means putting the clock back and reverting to infancy.

7. The law imposed a yoke of bondage; faith in Christ brings freedom. Why should sensible men who have been emancipated by Christ give up their freedom and submit afresh to servitude under the elemental powers through which the law was mediated? 'For freedom Christ has set us free; stand fast therefore, and do not submit again to a yoke of slavery' (Gal. v. 1).

8. Let it not be supposed that this freedom which the gospel of grace proclaims has any affinity with anarchic licence. The faith of which the gospel speaks is a faith which manifests itself outwardly in acts of love, and thus fulfils 'the law of Christ' (Gal. v. 6, vi. 2).

II. ASCETIC GNOSTICISM

Gnosticism is a mode of thought which we meet in a developed form in the second century. It reinterpreted Christianity for an intellectual élite by representing it as a form of higher 'knowledge' (*gnōsis*) by means of which the soul might be liberated from the shackles of the material order and mount to the upper realm of truth and light. In most Gnostic systems the disparagement of the material order manifested itself in severity to the human body; bodily asceticism and spiritual enrichment went together.

An incipient form of this Gnosticism is attacked by Paul in the Epistle to the Colossians. Colossae, a city in the Lycus valley in the province of Asia, had been evangelized by one of Paul's colleagues during Paul's three years of apostolic ministry in Ephesus (AD 52–55). A few years later, when Paul was in custody in Rome, waiting for his appeal to Caesar to be heard, news came to him of a disquieting development in the churches of the Lycus valley, and especially in the church of Colossae. There was a strong inclination on the part of that church to accept an attractive line of teaching which (although they did not suspect it) was calculated to subvert the pure gospel which they had believed and bring them into spiritual bondage.

Basically this teaching was Jewish. This seems clear from the place which it gave to legal ordinances, circumcision, food regulations, the sabbath, new moon and other prescriptions of the Jewish calendar. To this extent it was very similar to the legalism which Paul had previously had to deal with in the churches of Galatia. But on that Jewish foundation there had been raised a philosophical superstructure which was non-Jewish in origin. In this part of Asia Minor the barriers between the Jews and their pagan neighbours had ceased to be very effective. Social intermingling led to religious fusion, and the 'Colossian heresy' (as this teaching is commonly called) may be described as a Jewish-Hellenistic syncretism which had made room for some Christian elements in its system so as to attract the Christians in that region.

In this system the angelic or elemental power through which the Jewish law was given (cf. Acts vii. 53; Gal. iii. 19; Heb. ii. 2) was identified with the lords of the seven planetary spheres, 'principalities and powers' who had some share in the fullness of the divine nature and controlled the lines of communication between God and men. Since they were in a position to cut men off from access to God, tribute had to be paid to them in the form of law-keeping. To break the law meant incurring their resentment, and then they had to be appeased by severe self-denial and penance. In so far as this system paid any attention to the work of Christ, it probably suggested that His descent to earth and return to heaven could have taken place only by the permission of those powers; indeed, the fact of His suffering and death was probably regarded as evidence of His inferiority to them. Accordingly, allegiance to Christ was not a sufficient protection in a universe controlled by these mighty beings. That was clearly to be seen in the case of a man like Paul, one of the servants of Christ. The afflictions into which Paul was brought by his service to Christ showed that he had not attained that degree of control over the cosmic forces which would have enabled him to avoid all these afflictions.

This line of teaching appealed to a certain religious temperament, the more so as it claimed to be a form of advanced teaching for spiritually superior persons. Christians were invited to go in for this higher wisdom, to explore the hidden mysteries by a series of successive initiations until they reached perfection. Baptism was only a preliminary initiation; those who would pursue the path of truth further must put off all material elements by means of a rigorous asceticism until they were transported from this world of darkness to the domain of light, and so experienced full redemption.

But, however attractive this cult might be to many, Paul condemned it as specious make-believe. Far from representing a more advanced grade of knowledge than that provided by the apostolic gospel, it was completely inconsistent with that gospel and bade fair to undermine the foundations of Christianity. A system which exalted the planetary powers enthroned fate in place of the will of God; and a system which brought men into bondage to those powers denied the grace of God.

To this 'tradition of men', as he called it, Paul opposed the true tradition of Christ. The planetary powers have no part at all in the divine fullness; that fullness is perfectly embodied in Christ. In Christ all wisdom and knowledge are concentrated; in Christ all wisdom and knowledge are accessible to believers—not to a spiritual élite only, but to all. The planetary powers are not the mediators between God and men; that role is filled by Christ, who unites Godhead and manhood in His one Person. Was Christ inferior to the planetary powers? On the contrary; His supremacy over them is established by a twofold right. First, it was by Him and for Him that these powers were created, together with everything else that exists. Secondly, He vanquished them when they assaulted Him upon the cross, and by His victory over them He liberated from their now impotent grasp His people whom they had formerly held in bondage. Why should those who were united with Christ think it necessary to appease powers which owed their very existence to Him? And why should those who by faith had died and risen with Christ, thus sharing in His victory, pay any further tribute to powers which He had so signally defeated? Far from being an advanced form of wisdom, this angel-cult bore all the marks of immaturity; it called on those who had come of age in Christ to go back to the conditions of childhood.

In his defence of the gospel against this plausible theosophy, Paul gives a good example of his readiness to be 'all things to all men' for the gospel's sake (i Cor. ix. 22 f.). He confronts the false *gnōsis* and bodily asceticism which was being urged upon the Colossian Christians with the true *gnōsis* and spiritual asceticism of Christ. While he writes as an uncompromising opponent of the false teaching, he takes up its characteristic terms and shows how the truth which they attempt, unsuccessfully, to convey is embodied in Christ, the true 'mystery' (or revelation) of God.

In this Epistle Paul undertakes two apologetic tasks at once—the defence of Christianity over against the intellectual world of paganism and the defence of gospel truth within the church. As an apologist to the Gentiles, he was perhaps the first to meet his pagan opponents on their own ground and use their language in a Christian sense in order to make it clear that the problems to which they vainly sought an answer elsewhere found their satisfying solution in Christ.

His employment of the technical terms of the Colossian heresy in what has been called a 'disinfected' sense helps to explain the differences in vocabulary which have been observed between Colossians (and its sister-Epistle to the Ephesians) on the one hand and the rest of Paul's Epistles on the other hand. It may have been also in reaction to the Colossian heresy that Paul developed his earlier picture of the Christian fellowship in terms of the interrelated parts of the human body to the point reached in Colossians and Ephesians, where the Church is viewed as the body of which Christ is the Head. In this way he brings out not only the interdependence of the members of the believing community, but also the dependence of each and all of those members upon Christ for life and power; and he vindicates the supremacy of Christ against a system which would have cast Him down from His excellency.

In his reply to the Colossian heresy, Paul unfolds the cosmic significance of Christ more fully than he had done in his earlier writings. This theme is not absent from the earlier Epistles, but in Colossians and Ephesians it is expounded at length. While the teaching of justification by faith is the foundation of Paul's gospel, it does not exhaust his gospel. But in some quarters Paulinism has come to be identified so exclusively with this teaching, especially as expounded in Galatians and Romans, that the cosmic and corporate aspects of the gospel, as set forth in Colossians and Ephesians, have been felt to be un-Pauline. In fact, there is room in true Paulinism for both, and contemporary apologetic must also make room for both if it is not to be lopsided and defective.

For the truth of Christ's supremacy over all the powers in the universe is one which modern man sorely needs to learn. He is oppressed by a sense of impotence in the grasp of merciless forces which he can neither overcome nor escape. These forces may be Frankenstein monsters of man's own creation, or they may be horrors outside his conscious control; either way he is intimidated by the vastness of those fateful currents which threaten to sweep him on to destruction whether he will or no. And to modern man in his frustration and despair the full-orbed gospel of Christ, as Paul presents it to the Colossians, is the one message of hope. Christ crucified and risen is Lord of all; all the forces in the universe, well-disposed and ill-disposed, are subject to Him. To be united to Christ by faith is to throw off the thraldom of hostile powers, to enjoy perfect freedom, to gain the mastery over the dominion of evil because Christ's victory is ours.

III. ANTINOMIAN GNOSTICISM

While the view that matter was inherently evil led most Gnostics to treat the body with severity as a condition of saving the spirit of man, there were some Gnostic groups which argued differently. The body, they said, being part of the material order, is religiously irrelevant; whether it is treated roughly or indulgently makes no difference to one's spiritual well-being. This attitude could lead to a throwing off of restraint so far as the deeds of the body were concerned. For practical purposes the same end was served by those who argued that the body ought to be humiliated by being plunged in all sorts of vice and impurity.

By contrast with all these wrong attitudes to the body, the apostolic teaching lays it down that the body belongs to God as much as the spirit does, and should be dedicated to His service. But the one document in the New Testament which appears to deal most directly with the antinomian variety of Gnosticism, which refused restraint on the life of the body, is the tiny Epistle of Jude.

Jude, writing probably in the later part of the first century, tells his readers that when he was minded to write to them about 'our common salvation', he was constrained instead to use his pen in defence of the gospel against an insidious error which threatened to subvert it. But Jude by no means confined himself to passive defence. There are times when it is not enough to hold and expound the truth; the war must be carried into the enemy's lines so that the error may be attacked, exposed and refuted.

The faith for which Jude contends is 'the faith which was once for all delivered to the saints'. It was delivered by the Lord to His apostles, and by them to His people. For Christ is God's complete Word to men; He has nothing to say which has not been said in Christ. Therefore all claims to convey an *additional* revelation to that which has been given in Christ (as distinct from bringing out the fuller implications of the revelation in Christ) are false claims. That is so whether these claims are embodied in books which aim at superseding or supplementing the Bible, or take the form of extra-biblical traditions which are promulgated as dogmas by ecclesiastical authority. It is true, as John Robinson said, that 'the Lord hath more truth yet to break forth out of His holy Word'; but that truth will break forth from the Word already spoken, the Word which became incarnate in Jesus Christ and has been recorded for us in Holy Writ. The Spirit of God, who spoke by the prophets and apostles, still speaks to us through their words and thus bears witness to Christ, the perfect revelation of God.

The false teachers against whom Jude defends the faith had not launched their attack upon it as open enemies, but had infiltrated into the Christian position. They had professed faith in Christ, received baptism in His name, entered into church fellowship, but were revealed by their conduct to be wolves in sheep's clothing. They took advantage of the pardoning message of the gospel as though the efficacy of Christ's redemptive work gave them licence to sin as they pleased, without fear of consequences. Like some people whom Paul knew, and like Rasputin in our own century, they considered that they ought to continue in sin, that grace might abound. By so doing, says Jude, they 'pervert the grace of our God into licentiousness'. Their lives showed them to be utter strangers to the meaning and power of the gospel, and constituted an open denial of Christ. When Jude says that they 'deny our only Master and Lord, Jesus Christ', he may have their moral teachings and practices in mind; but these teachings and practices were probably attended by a false conception of the Person and work of Christ, such as appears one way or another in all the Gnostic systems.

How does Jude defend the faith against the dangers which these people presented to it?

Firstly, he reminds his readers of Old Testament characters in whose succession these false teachers run. Just as the judgment of God fell on the rebellious Israelites in the wilderness, on the disobedient angels, on the inhabitants of the cities of the plain, just as it fell on individuals like Cain, Balaam and Korah, so it would fall on these. Those Old Testament characters revolted against God and His representatives and suffered for it; so these false teachers disregarded the custodians of godly order in the churches and fed themselves instead of their misguided followers.

Secondly, Jude points out that these false teachers were foreseen by the Old Testament prophets and by the apostles of Christ, who issued warnings in advance against their plausible devices. Indeed, he finds in them a fulfilment of the predictions about Antichrist; when he describes them as 'loud-mouthed boasters' (verse 16), he uses language borrowed from Daniel's description of the wilful king who would 'speak astonishing things against the God of gods' (Dn. xi. 36). Nor was Jude the only Christian writer around that time to recognize in heretics preliminary manifestations of the spirit of Antichrist which was to be unleashed at the time of the end (cf. 1 Jn. ii. 18, 22, iv. 3; 2 Jn. 7).

Thirdly, Jude exhorts his readers to make the apostolic faith the foundation of their lives, to persevere in prayer, to abide in the fellowship of God's love and to look forward to that outpouring of mercy which would mark the second advent of Christ. Thus their feet would be kept in the way leading to eternal life. Let them at the same time rescue those who were in danger of being misled by the false teachers, while abhorring the false teaching itself.

And fourthly, he commends them to God, who is able to guard His people from stumbling until at last He brings them into His own glorious presence and satisfies them with His joy. For all the vigour of his polemic, he does not content himself with the denunciation of error, but finds the best defence against its insidious approaches in a closer adherence to the love of God and faith in Christ.

IV. DOCETISM

The Gnostic view of the material world as unreal or as essentially evil ran counter to several of the basic tenets of the New Testament faith. It undermined the doctrine of creation, for something which was unreal or essentially evil could not have been made by God. It undermined the doctrine of the incarnation, for obviously the divine Being could not inhabit a material body if the substance of that body was unreal or evil. One attempt to reconcile the Gnostic doctrine of matter with the apostolic teaching about Christ was the theory that the body which our Lord took at His coming into the world was not a real body but a phantom one. He only *seemed* to inhabit a material body, and from the Greek word *dokein,* which means 'to seem', people who held this theory were known as Docetists.

But if Christ's incarnation was unreal, His death and resurrection were also unreal; and the whole gospel message was thus evacuated of its truth and power. One unhappy legacy of this short-lived phase of Christian heresy (short-lived so far as its career within the history of Christianity is concerned) remains to bedevil Christian witness to Muslims up to the present day. For when the Koran says of Jesus that 'they did not kill Him, nor did they crucify Him, but they *thought* they did', we may infer that Muhammad was indebted for this idea to a Christian source tainted with docetism.

Towards the end of the first century, then, we find Christian communities receiving repeated warnings against those who denied the reality of Christ's incarnation—who denied His coming in the flesh. These people might occupy a vantage-point as prophets, whose unpremeditated words were commonly believed to be words prompted by the Spirit of God. Christians had to be warned that it was only by the content of the words spoken by these prophets that it could be decided whether they were prompted by the Spirit of God or by a spirit of a very different sort. At the beginning of the second century Ignatius, bishop of Antioch, in spite of the fact that he possessed the gift of prophecy himself, found it necessary to curb its exercise in the churches because it was being misused to gain a hearing for false teaching. And earlier still, John the Evangelist (if we may ascribe the Johannine Epistles as well as the Gospel to him) finds it necessary to write to Christians in Asia Minor : 'Beloved, do not believe every spirit, but test the spirits to see whether they are of God; for many false prophets have gone out into the world. By this you know the Spirit of God : every spirit which confesses that Jesus Christ has come in the flesh is of God, and every spirit which does not confess Jesus is not of God' (1 Jn. iv. 1 ff.). And again : 'Many deceivers have gone out into the world, men who will not acknowledge the coming of Jesus Christ in the flesh; such a one is the deceiver and the antichrist' (2 Jn. 7).

One form of docetic teaching is associated with the name of Cerinthus, who according to tradition was the 'deceiver' whom John had specially in mind. Cerinthus, we are told, held that 'the Christ' (a divine power) descended on the man Jesus when he was baptized and enabled him to perform the mighty works which characterized his ministry, but left him before his death. This last point is well illustrated by the so-called *Gospel of Peter,* a docetic document of the second century, which represents Jesus as crying out on the cross : 'My power, my power, why hast thou left me ?'

John refutes this teaching explicitly both in his Gospel and in his Epistles. When in 1 Jn. v. 6 he says, 'This is he who came by water and blood, Jesus Christ, not with the water only but with the water and the blood,' he is thinking of those who held that the Christ came with water (i.e. at the time of Jesus' baptism) but not with the blood (because the divine power abandoned Him before His death). Some commentators see in these words of

John a reference to the two Christian sacraments, and they may not be wrong in this; but John is primarily concerned with historical realities which lie behind the sacraments. He who was baptized was Christ, the Son of God; He who died was Christ, the Son of God. He replies to the docetic distortion of the faith with a positive affirmation of the true doctrine of Christ.

Similarly in his Gospel he speaks of our Lord's incarnation in language too direct and unambiguous to be misunderstood or misinterpreted in a docetic sense : 'the Word became flesh' (Jn. i. 14). Had he said that 'the Word assumed manhood' or 'took to Himself a human body' he would have spoken the truth, but with the blunt assertion that the Word *became* flesh he insisted on the reality of the incarnation in terms which could not be used as a convenient theological formula covering a wide variety of interpretations.

And as he emphasizes the reality of the incarnation at the beginning of his Gospel, so towards the end of his Gospel he asserts the reality of the death of Christ against those who held that He only seemed to die, or that it was not the Christ who died. In his narrative of the crucifixion he describes how, after Jesus had died, His side was pierced by a spear, 'and at once there came out blood and water' (Jn. xix. 34). Then he adds : 'He who saw it has borne witness—his testimony is true, and he knows that he tells the truth—that you also may believe.' This solemn attestation is evidently intended to confirm (*a*) that Christ really died, (*b*) that by His death the Old Testament prophecies regarding the Messiah were fulfilled, and (*c*) that the blood and water which came from His side were a parabolic token of the truth that He came 'not with the water only but with the water and the blood'.

The historical facts about Christ are our court of appeal both for the rebuttal of error and for the establishment of truth. No pronouncement by ecclesiastical authority can carry such weight as these do. 'Councils, we admit, and Creeds, cannot go behind, but must wholly rest upon the history of our Lord Jesus Christ.'[1]

The presentation of the gospel in all its fullness and depth is the best defence against pseudo-Christianity. So evidently the apostles and other first-century Christians believed. The refutation of error, they knew, was necessary, but only so that the ground might be cleared for the proclamation of the truth.

Some of the deviations with which they had to deal are still with us. The most perennially popular is that which imagines that we can win acceptance with God by our own works, or simply by our ordinary decent nature. What more could God want? I suppose several of us have had the experience of explaining justification by faith to someone in words of one syllable, so as to make it crystal-clear—only to be told at the end : 'Yes, that's what I always say : we must just do the best we can.' Man's bankruptcy before God, his utter indebtedness to God's free grace, the all-sufficiency of Christ—these foundations of the gospel need to be insisted upon today as much as they did when Paul wrote his Epistle to the Galatians. But if any should mistakenly conclude that the Christian liberty into which the grace of God brings us means freedom from ethical obligations, then there is great need to insist that, on the contrary, the grace of God trains us 'to renounce irreligion and worldly passions, and to live sober, upright, and godly lives' (Tit. ii. 12). And when an attempt is made to 'restate' Christianity in terms of some current philosophical or cosmological fashion, in such a way that it ceases to be genuine Christianity, let us remember that the first Christian century was acquainted with such attempts and learned how to deal with them. Philosophical and cosmological fashions tend to be ephemeral. If Christianity had in fact become completely identified with first-century fashions of this kind, it would speedily have become obsolete. The everlasting gospel is not tied

[1] R . C. Moberly, *Lux Mundi*, p. 117.

to out-of-date world-views; it is relevant to every age, to the twentieth century as much as to the first, because it meets the total need of man through Jesus Christ, who is the same yesterday and today and forever.

CHAPTER V

THE FINALITY OF THE GOSPEL

THE relevance of the subject of this chapter is underlined by the following press report which appeared in various places early in April 1958:

> A native evangelist on the Danish mission field in the Sudan has been fined and sentenced to six months' imprisonment for having offended the Muslims by delivering a sermon on the words of Jesus: 'No man cometh unto the Father but by me.' The evangelist has maintained that he said nothing hostile to the Muslim faith, and has lodged an appeal. At the same time three Sudanese pastors and one church member were imprisoned, but were acquitted. Danish mission circles report that the matter has aroused great attention, and further developments are being closely watched.

I have no information which would throw light on the accuracy of this report, or on the circumstances of the incident reported. But it does bring home to us what, to many people's minds, is the crucial *skandalon* of the Christian faith, its central offence. Christianity will not come to terms with other religions, nor will it relax its exclusive claims so as to countenance or accommodate them. It presents itself, as it did in the first century, as God's final word to man; it proclaims Christ, as it did in the first century, to be the one Mediator between God and man. The Sudanese evangelist might be right in maintaining that he said nothing hostile to the Muslim faith so far as the law of the land was concerned, but in a religious sense any proclamation of the gospel, especially when based on such a text as he chose, must inevitably be hostile to a system which proclaims another than Christ to be the spokesman of God *par excellence*.

The apologetic of the New Testament is set in a world-view which is biblical through and through. We

have seen how this world-view was presented in the
apostolic defence of the gospel against first-century
paganism. In it God is set forth as Creator of the world,
Sustainer of life, Lord of history, and Judge of all.
Christ, the Son of God, occupies a central place in this
world-view : He is the one through whom all things
were created, in whom all things cohere as He upholds
them by His enabling word, who by His triumph over
evil has proved Himself to be Lord of history, and who
has been designated by God as Judge of the living and
the dead. And this Christ appeared on earth 'once for
all, at the consummation of the ages, to put away sin
by his self-sacrifice' (see Heb. ix. 26). It is not that the
consummation of the ages was the time when, in fact,
He appeared; it is rather that His coming and achieve-
ment made that particular time the consummation of
the ages. In Him the biblical world-view is presented in
eschatological terms, and in this way the finality of
God's revelation in Him is emphasized.

There are two New Testament documents which, in
different ways, bring out the finality of Christianity, and
we can best understand this aspect of Christian apologetic in the first century by paying some attention to
them. They are the Epistle to the Hebrews and the
Gospel of John.

I. THE EPISTLE TO THE HEBREWS

In 1899 a distinguished Scottish theologian, A. B. Bruce,
produced a book under the title, *The Epistle to the
Hebrews: The First Apology for Christianity*. Whether
the term 'first' in the sub-title is completely justified is a
matter for debate, but apart from that the sub-title
states concisely what the Epistle to the Hebrews really
is. The unknown author's aim, as Bruce puts it in his
preface, was 'to show the excellence of Christianity to
a community possessing a very defective insight into its
true nature'.

The circumstances which called forth this Epistle

must be inferred from its contents, and different infer-
ences have been drawn by different readers. One of the
most convincing accounts of the matter known to me
is that presented in William Manson's Baird lectures,
The Epistle to the Hebrews (1951). According to him,
the Epistle (which is rather a homily in written form,
with a few personal notes added at the end) was
addressed to a group of Christians of Jewish origin,
domiciled probably in Rome. These Christians were
inclined to look back instead of forward; they hesitated
to detach themselves completely from Judaism and commit themselves unreservedly to the onward march of the
people of God. They were even in danger of giving up
the faith which they had once placed in Christ, partly
because of persecution and disillusionment, and partly
(perhaps) because they were influenced by 'diverse and
strange teachings' similar to those which were finding
their way into the Colossian church. One or two recent
writers have seen affinities between positions criticized in
the Epistle to the Hebrews and positions attested in the
Qumran documents; but all that can be said on this
score is that the Jewish communities in Rome preserved
certain features which we asssociate with the baptist
sects of the Jordan valley and Dead Sea region rather
than with normative Judaism.

The people to whom the Epistle is addressed were
tempted to discontinue their Christian fellowship with
its forward-looking challenge, and lose their identity
within Judaism. The writer therefore insists upon the
finality of the Christian revelation, the imminent dis-
appearance of the old Jewish order, the irrevocable
doom incurred by apostasy, and the blessedness of the
Christian hope.

Many of the details of his argument are specially
applicable to the situation with which he was dealing.
For this reason it has sometimes been suggested that his
argument is not generally applicable to the present day.
According to a recent evangelical American expositor,
'the entire book is concerned with a situation that

obtained in the first century which does not exist today'
and therefore, while the primary application of the
Epistle must be determined from a study of its historical
background and analysis, 'there can be no secondary
application for today, since the conditions which existed
then do not obtain today'. To which it may be said in
reply that the general argument of the Epistle is valid
and applicable wherever the people of God are in danger
of losing their faith in Him and slipping back instead
of pressing on.

Here is a summary of the argument of the Epistle :

'God spoke in various ways to our fathers through the
prophets, but now He has spoken His final word to us in
His Son, His perfect image. The Son of God is greater
than any prophet; He is greater even than the angels, as
the Old Testament scriptures amply testify. It was
through angels that Moses' law was communicated, and
its sanctions were severe enough; how much more
perilous must it be to ignore the saving message brought
by no angel, but by Jesus, the Son of God!

'Jesus, the Son of God, is the One to whom the
dominion of the world has been committed for all time
to come. As the eighth psalm teaches us, God has put
everything under the dominion of man, and it was the
nature of man—*our* nature—that the Son of God took
upon Himself in order to win back this dominion,
conquer the devil who had usurped it, and rescue those
whom he held in bondage. It is because Jesus became
truly man, moreover, that He is qualified to act as High
Priest on His people's behalf : He knows all their trials
from His own experience and therefore can give them
the timely help they need. (Only, let us beware. Those
who rebelled against God in the days of the wilderness
wanderings were excluded from His rest in the promised
land. But there is a better rest than the rest which the
Israelites found in Canaan; it is the rest which still
awaits the people of God, and we must take care not to
forfeit that rest by rebelling against God when He speaks

to us no longer through Moses, as He did in those days, but through His Son, a greater than Moses.)

'As has been said, Jesus is our great High Priest, able to sympathize with His people and help them. We may safely look for understanding and delivering grace to the One who endured the agonies of Gethsemane. He has been called to His high-priestly office by God Himself, as an Old Testament oracle makes clear: "The LORD has sworn and will not change his mind, Thou art a priest for ever, after the order of Melchizedek." (I should like to enlarge on this point, but really I do not know if I can; you are so immature in your Christianity. I must warn you solemnly that those who have once been baptized and tasted the blessings of the new age can never repeat the experience of repentance and regeneration if they commit apostasy. Not that I think you really mean to be apostates; I have better hopes of you than that. I want you rather to press on from the point you have reached, so as to attain full maturity instead of sticking at that point, or slipping back.)

'Christ, then, is by divine appointment a High Priest of Melchizedek's order. You remember the story of Melchizedek, priest of God Most High (Gn. xiv. 18 ff.). He appears suddenly, without antecedents, and nothing is said about his subsequent career. Yet he was a very great man; our father Abraham paid him tithes, and received his blessing. You might even say that Levi, ancestor of the priestly families of Israel, paid Melchizedek tithes in the person of his great-grandfather Abraham. This implies that Melchizedek is greater than Levi, and Melchizedek's priesthood better than Aaron's. And indeed that is obvious, for if perfection was to be attained under the Aaronic priesthood, why should God have conferred on the Messiah a priesthood of a different line?

'In many ways Jesus' priesthood after Melchizedek's order is superior to Aaron's priesthood. Jesus is immortal, whereas the priests of Aaron's line die one by one. Jesus is sinless, whereas the priests of Aaron's line have to present a sin-offering for themselves before they can present one for the people. *Their* sacrificial service must constantly be repeated, because it is never really effective; Jesus, by the single sacrifice of Himself, put away His people's sin for ever. They ministered under the old covenant instituted at Mount Sinai; Jesus is the Mediator of the new covenant—the covenant whose inauguration Jeremiah foretold. The fact that it is a new covenant means that the former one is obsolete. They minister in an earthly sanctuary belonging to the old order, where a thick curtain bars the way to the divine presence; Jesus exercises *His* high priesthood in the heavenly sanctuary, where there is no such barrier between the worshippers and God. And this heavenly sanctuary where we have such direct access to God is the real sanctuary, of which the earthly one was only a copy. For the old Judaism compared to the Christian revelation is as shadow to substance.

'Let us, then, abandon the old, obsolescent order and approach God along this new way which Jesus by His death has opened up for us. Let us maintain steadfast hope and faith in Him. In this way we shall have a firm assurance of those eternal realities which cannot be seen with outward eyesight; we shall be able to look forward with eager hope to the certain coming of the Coming One. It was by such forward-looking faith that the saints of earlier days won the approval of God; let us follow their example. Better still, let us follow the example of Jesus Himself, for He ran the race of faith steadfastly, despite all the shame of the cross, and He is now enthroned at God's right hand. Don't let us grow fainthearted because of our trials : these trials are a proof that we really *are* God's sons. And think of the glory to which we have been introduced in this new age of fulfilment—something far surpassing what men of faith experienced in days gone by. How could we ever think of going back to imperfect and obsolete forms of worship?

'So, then, maintain your Christian confession in

patience and hope; live as Christians should; and may God, who raised Jesus from the dead, help you to do His will in all things.'

Such is the writer's argument, and it must be readily conceded that many of its details could play little part in Christian apologetic today. But when we look beyond the immediate circumstances which evoked this first-century defence of the faith, the peculiar and temporary dilemma in which its first readers found themselves, and consider its central emphasis, we may recognize an abiding validity in its argument.

The writer insists that Christ is God's final word to man. Those who neglect or abandon the way of life in Christ can expect no further message from God, no new way of salvation which will bring them pardon or peace apart from Christ's sacrifice of Himself, presented once for all. This note, 'once for all', pervades the whole Epistle, pointing readers to 'the finished work of Christ' as the one adequate basis for their faith. Here, we are assured, is something to cleanse and reassure the conscience with a thoroughness matched by nothing else in the world.

But while His saving work was accomplished once for all, Jesus Christ abides for evermore, 'the same yesterday and today and for ever' (Heb. xiii. 8). Everything else changes; religious fashions come and go; leaders and teachers die; heaven and earth pass away. 'But thou art the same, and thy years will never end' : so said an ancient psalmist (see Ps. cii. 27) in words which our author applies to Jesus (Heb. i. 12). Jesus therefore provides the one stable foundation for faith.

But this does not imply a static attitude of mind. On the contrary, this Epistle repeatedly calls on the people of God to press forward. 'Let us go on! Let us go forth!' 'We must pay the closer attention to what we have heard, lest we drift away from it' (Heb. ii. 1). Jesus, so to speak, represents the fixed point on the bank; we are carried down past Him on the stream of time, unless we continually press on, rowing upstream so as to keep alongside Him. Or we may change the figure and say with James Russell Lowell :

> New occasions teach new duties;
>   Time makes ancient good uncouth;
> They must upward still and onward
>   Who would keep abreast of truth.

Christians are Christians by virtue of certain acts of God which took place at a definite time in the past, but these acts of God have released a dynamic force which will never allow Christians to stay put or stick in the mud. The faith once for all delivered to the saints is not something which we can catch and tame; it is something which is always leading us forth to new ventures in the cause of Christ, as God calls afresh. It was because of Abraham's firm faith in the unchanging God that he was so ready to go forth at God's bidding, not knowing where he might be led. To stay at the point to which some revered teacher of the past brought us, out of a mistaken sense of loyalty to him; to continue to follow a certain pattern of religious activity just because it was good enough for our fathers and grandfathers— these and the like are temptations which make the message of Hebrews a necessary and salutary one for us to listen to. Every new movement of the Spirit of God tends to become stereotyped in the next generation, and what we have heard with our ears, what our fathers have told us, becomes a tenacious tradition encroaching on the allegiance which ought to be accorded only to the living and active Word of God. As the Christian surveys the world of today, he sees very much land to be possessed in the name of Christ, but to take possession of it calls for a generous measure of that forward-looking faith which is so earnestly urged upon the readers of the Epistle to the Hebrews. Those first readers were living at a time when the old, cherished order was breaking up. Attachment to the venerable traditions of the past

could avail them nothing in this situation; only attachment to the unchanging and onward-moving Christ
could carry them forward and enable them to face the
new order with confidence and power. So, in a day when
everything that can be shaken is being shaken before
our eyes and beneath our feet, let us give thanks for the
unshakable kingdom which we have inherited, which
endures for ever when everything else that men's hopes
may be pinned to disappears and leaves not a wrack
behind.

II. THE GOSPEL OF JOHN

Towards the end of the first Christian century, Christianity had established its position in the Roman world,
and especially round the shores of the Eastern Mediter-
ranean, as a faith and life distinct from Judaism, with
which it had historically so close an association. The
original setting of the gospel story—Palestine as it was
forty years before the end of the Second Jewish Commonwealth—was now a thing of the past. Since Christianity was a faith based on historical events, the
terminology in which it was habitually presented had
inevitable links with that by-gone epoch. Was a faith
whose origin was so closely tied to a particular place
and a particular time really relevant for other places
and other times?

This is the situation to which the last survivor of Jesus'
closest companions addresses himself in the Fourth
Gospel. He cannot and will not depart from the historic
foundation of the gospel message—the place and time
at which the saving events took place—but he will
present that message, he will record those events, in a
form which will bring out their permanent significance.
He considers himself first and foremost as a witness—a
witness to things which he and his companions saw and
heard in Palestine in the third decade of the century.
But he records his witness in such a way that people in
the wider Hellenistic world of the last decade of the

century, whether Jews or Gentiles, may share something of what he and his friends experienced as they saw the glory of God shining in the life of 'Jesus of Nazareth, the son of Joseph'. And, in fact, so admirably has he achieved his purpose that a far wider world than that for which he wrote, the world of the twentieth century, can still sit at his feet as he portrays the Life which was the light of men, and find itself face to face with the eternal Christ.

The Gospel of John incidentally includes various phases of apologetic. We have already noted its defence of the historic gospel against the Docetists; it defends it also against objections from the side of Judaism, and possibly even against criticisms voiced by people who continued to look upon John the Baptist as the greatest of teachers sent from God and not as the forerunner of a greater than himself. And John moves easily from defensive apologetic to positive polemic; the 'disciple whom Jesus loved' is impatient of compromise, and those who do not share his estimate of his Master have a black mark placed against them, whether they are outright enemies or temporizers who, for fear of the authorities, fail to appear openly as His disciples, preferring the praise of men to the praise of God.

But these apologetic and polemic motifs are caught up into the Evangelist's overriding purpose, which is to bear witness to Jesus as the incarnation of God's eternal Word, the self-expression of God in a very real human life lived on the plane of this world's history. The Word, the *logos,* of God came to men in a variety of forms in earlier days, but in Jesus it became flesh. God could not bring His Word home to men more closely than in a real life lived in their midst; therefore, with the coming of Jesus, God's revelation is complete.

'The Word became flesh,' says John, 'and pitched His tabernacle in our midst, and we beheld His glory.' How the divine glory was seen in Jesus is the theme of the Gospel; John records a succession of mighty works from the ministry of Jesus which he presents as 'signs'—signs,

that is, of the divine glory which was revealed in Him.
At the marriage-feast in Cana and at the sepulchre of
Lazarus, on the Galilaean hillside and in the temple
court at Jerusalem, and supremely in His death upon
the cross and His rising from the tomb Jesus manifests
the glory of God to those who have eyes to see.

As these signs are recorded, one after another, the
lessons which they symbolize are impressed upon the
reader. Jesus is the true sustainer of the life of men—
He is the bread of life and supplies the water of life.
The restricted worship of earlier days has given place
in Him to a new order where, without limitations of
space or time, men may worship the Father in spirit and
in truth. Compared with this new order, the old is as
water over against the wine into which He has trans-
muted it. The old liturgy, the sacred year punctuated by
the festivals with their historic associations, reminding
the people of what God did for their fathers in days gone
by—all this has now been summed up in the new
revelation and the new deliverance wrought by God in
Christ.

And this is brought out in such a way as to make it
plain that Gentile believers in Christ have as full and
rightful a share in all the blessings which He bestows as
Jewish believers have. The line of demarcation between
Israel and the nations belonged to the order now past.
When, a few days before His crucifixion, some Greeks
who were present at the passover celebrations expressed
a desire to see Jesus, the answer which He gave implied
that very soon they would have as much free access to
Him as ever the men and women of His own nation
could have: 'and I, when I am lifted up from the earth,
will draw all men to myself' (Jn. xii. 32)—all men without distinction, Gentiles and Jews alike. Sometimes
writers on the problem of the Fourth Gospel have
grappled with the question whether it was intended for
Jewish readers or for Gentile readers. But surely it was
intended for both, written that Jew and Gentile alike
might believe that Jesus is the Christ, the Son of God,

and by believing might have life in His name (Jn. xx. 31).

The last word from the cross which this Evangelist records is 'It is finished' (Jn. xix. 30); and it is a word which sums up much of what he emphasizes throughout the Gospel. In Jesus all the will of God is accomplished, all the revelation of God, all the promises of God. God had sent His Word on many occasions in the past, but all that He had said on those earlier occasions was summed up and perfected in the unfolding of His glory seen in the passion and triumph of Christ. His crucifixion is described by John as His 'being lifted up'—a term which is designedly ambiguous, for it denotes at one and the same time His literal 'lifting up' on the cross and His exaltation by God.

John, in fact, is saying in his way what the writer to the Hebrews says in another way. The first three verses of Hebrews could be regarded as a summary of John's Gospel. What God said formerly to the fathers through the prophets has now been consummated in His final utterance in His Son. But while the writer to the Hebrews conveys his message in the form of a homily, a 'word of exhortation' (Heb. xiii. 22), John conveys his in the form of a narrative. His narrative is unmistakably the primitive apostolic preaching, presented so that its abiding relevance may be appreciated. The long course of God's revelation of Himself to the world reached its consummation, he says, at a particular place and time, under well-defined historical circumstances.

Pilate, Roman procurator of Judaea from AD 26 to 36, who handed Jesus over to be crucified, 'wrote a title and put it on the cross; it read, "Jesus of Nazareth, the King of the Jews" . . . and it was written in Hebrew, in Latin, and in Greek' (Jn. xix. 19 f.). When the Jewish chief priests protested against his choice of words, he answered, 'What I have written I have written' (Jn. xix. 22). And in reporting Pilate's answer, John probably intends us to realize that the wording had an even greater permanence than Pilate himself envisaged.

But what could it matter to Hellenistic readers at the end of the first century who was King of the Jews in AD 30? If that was the charge on which Jesus was put to death, how could His death have significance for them? John foresees this difficulty, and prepares his readers for it. In his account of Pilate's examination of Jesus, he narrates something which the other Evangelists do not narrate, and which helps to explain Pilate's otherwise inexplicable reluctance to ratify the Sanhedrin's death-sentence without much ado. The Sanhedrin charged Jesus before Pilate with claiming to be King of the Jews. 'So,' says Pilate, 'you are King of the Jews, are you?' 'I *am* a king,' says Jesus, 'but not in a sense that you would recognize. If I were a king in the ordinary sense, claiming an earthly kingdom, My followers would be fighting in My defence. But My kingdom is the kingdom of truth; My subjects are those who love truth, and I am their King.' No wonder that Pilate interjected 'What is truth?' and broke off the investigation.

But if it did not matter very much to Hellenistic readers at the end of the first century who was King of the Jews sixty years before, it ought to matter very much to them whether they recognized God's truth or not. There are those who ask 'What is truth?' in a detached manner, and try to discover the answer without personal commitment. But there are those who seek for truth with passionate urgency, determined to commit themselves wholeheartedly to it, if only they can find it. To them the promise of Jesus comes true : 'Seek and you will find.' For He comes to them in person and says : 'I am the truth.' And here is something which is relevant to men and women in every century. Because the Word became flesh, suffered for us men and for our salvation 'under Pontius Pilate' and is alive for evermore, eternal truth has drawn near to us in Him. In Him God has come to us; by Him we may come to God. Every word of God that has come to men has come through Him (whether men have been aware of it or not); every prayer of man that has reached the heart of God has done so through

Him (whether men have been aware of it or not). However the gospel may be defended, it cannot be defended by concessions which deprive it of its essence or detract from our Saviour's title to be called The Word of God. Christian apologetic today as in the first century must echo His own affirmation : 'I am the way, and the truth, and the life; no one comes to the Father, but by me' (Jn. xiv. 6). God's approach to man is embodied in Love incarnate; and that same Love incarnate embodies man's approach to God.

REFERENCES TO EARLY LITERATURE

INDEX OF SCRIPTURE REFERENCES